To my wife Kathy with all my love.

Warm Beer, Lousy Food

The Crazy Country Club

John S. Columbia

iUniverse, Inc.
New York Bloomington

Warm Beer, Lousy Food
The Crazy Country Club

iUniverse books may be ordered through booksellers or by contacting:

iUniverse
1663 Liberty Drive
Bloomington, IN 47403
www.iuniverse.com
1-800-Authors (1-800-288-4677)

Because of the dynamic nature of the Internet, any Web addresses or links contained in this book may have changed since publication and may no longer be valid.

ISBN: 978-1-4401-7175-8 (sc)
ISBN: 978-1-4401-7177-2 (dj)
ISBN: 978-1-4401-7176-5 (ebk)

Printed in the United States of America

iUniverse rev. date: 11/20/2009

Acknowledgements

I'd like to thank my wife Kathy, and family and friends, who encouraged me to undertake the writing of this book. I want to thank Dianne Steinberg for her invaluable aid. I am eternally grateful. To my son John, who, despite my ignorance of the computer, saw me through every problem I incurred. He also designed the cover of this book, and in it caught the flavor of what the Club was all about. Last but certainly not least, I want to thank both Lou and Tony Burdo for their help, in both furnishing some of the photos, stories and memories that make up this book. And to all the guys mentioned in the book, what a great time we had. Thanks to Larry, Nibs, Carl and Andy. Stewie, Little Tony, Stevie Shades and Big Dick. To those who are no longer here; Tommy, Pete, Moose, Otto, Cappy, Crazy Tony and Sal Da Doorman. To everyone that ever bussed a table and cracked a joke while they did it. I am and will always be grateful to have worked with you. You are *the Cream of the Crap*. Louie, this one's for you.

Preface

This is the remarkable story of how Lou Burdo turned a run down bar into a viable business that lasted forty five years. What makes it so impressive, is that without the benefit of agents or advertising to any great degree, he built a place so unique and entertaining, that someone just had to tell the story.

I had the pleasure of sharing a weekend stage with Lou for twelve years, and I can tell you that the laughs never stopped. Ask anyone in Brooklyn about the *Crazy Country Club* and you'll get a different story from each of them. No one agreed on what they had heard or saw such was the volume of material thrown their way The one common thread shared by all was that The Crazy Country Club was very unusual, and always a riot.

This is to all the guys I worked with and to all the good times. This is for all the weddings that I had to miss, and for all the gratitude that I feel for having had the opportunity to work in such a jocular environment.

To think, that such a conglomeration of men, with backgrounds so varied, could come together and produce shows that kept them rolling in the aisles week after week, is quite astounding. The way that Lou molded our untrained talent, was undertaken by him with an attitude that never intimidated or embarrassed us. I never felt in jeopardy when he was beside me on stage. If anyone committed a flub during the show, he'd always be there to bail us out.

I think the genius behind the operation was that the waiters and bartenders were just regular guys who could be your next door neighbor, without the outrageous behavior and dress that many times goes hand and hand with the entertainment world. When the construction worker or the carpenter walked into the club to work, everything became null and void except for the desire to make people laugh. We all wanted to be part of something bigger, something that just might last a lifetime. What a wonderful feeling it is to be recognized twenty years after working your last show and hearing what a great time everyone had.

Lou once told me, that if he ever wrote a book about the Club, he'd call it *The Cream of the Crap*. Personally, I think the name he gave the Club fits it perfectly. Here's the story of *Warm Beer and Lousy Food*.

Contents

Chapter 1

New Years Eve

New Years Eve, 1965, proved to be a cold and bitter night and the streets of Brooklyn showed signs of freezing over. *The Country Club* was decked out in its holiday finest, and the air was festive with Carol's being sung.

Santa Claus sat against the bar nursing his Gin and Tonic. As he plucked on the strings of his standup bass, Louie, sitting near him strummed his guitar. Larry made a great Santa as he was six foot tall and two hundred and seventy pounds. Louie was dressed in a fine holiday style; purple turtle neck with white suspenders, and together they sang.

Christmas lights and colored glass balls hung everywhere, seemingly placed without thought or design. For a brief moment the setting seemed normal. Then the door opened.

A blast of cold air caught the bartender by surprise, and instinctively he shouted, "Close the frigging door...you're freezing my balls off."

As he spoke he held up and shook a small Christmas tree bedecked with ornaments. Some of them flew off and crashed to the floor. Some of the patrons laughed along with *Tommy, a/k/a, Uncle Festus, Mr. Clean.*

The ceiling seemed to sway as many of the plastic arms and legs and other paraphernalia caught the breeze. The thousands of objects that were nailed, screwed and wired to the walls and ceiling, were hard to digest, and your eyes went into a confused state just trying to absorb it all. The Christmas tinsel made everything shine like the stars leading the three wise men to find God. One thing the Club wasn't was a church. Actually there was a large Baptist Church across the street and the story was that Louie actually had to count the distance from church to bar in feet, front door to front door, in order to be legal. He covered the distance with less than a foot to spare. We were never any competition for the church, because people didn't come to the Club to pray, they came to laugh.

"Table of four," Sal the Doorman yelled.

"They look like more then four to me," said Louie.

The juke box was playing but not so loud that it interfered with hearing the remarks from the help. *The song was a 1963 hit called Walk Right In recorded by the Rooftop Singers.* The song was still popular and although the words held little content, it was easy to sing along with. As it played the waiters sang along with it inviting the customers in. They sang,
Walk right in, sit right down,
Daddy let your mind roll on,
Walk right in, sit right down,
Daddy let your mind roll on,
Everybody's talking 'bout a new way of walking,
Do you want to lose your mind?
Walk right in, sit right down, Daddy let your mind roll on.

Louie stood up and approached the foursome strumming his guitar. Santa followed as did the other waiters. The Juke Box mysteriously lost volume as they began to sing,

"Walk right in, sit down and squat,
Don't forget to hit the bowl,
Walk right in, everything's hot,
We never let the seat get cold,

Now you look like you're down on your luck,
Why don't you shake your ass, we'll all make a buck,

So walk right in, sit down and squat,
Don't forget to hit the bowl...

The song trailed off with laughter from both the help and the customer's. The man leading the way was heavier than his wife, but non-the-less, she was a big women.

Pointing to the ceiling he turned to his friend and said, "Ya see... there's the jockstrap they dropped on my head."

The second couple, both tall and thin, looked about the room in disbelief. As the heavy man ran his hands around his waistband in order to heist up his pants, a large sombrero dropped on top of him and a loud whistle blew. The Mexican hat was almost four feet across and engulfed two of them. Startled, they jumped away from it and an air horn went off directly below them. The air was hooked up to a giant compressor in the cellar, and both of the women's dresses flew high. The ladies fought to keep them down. The fat man laughed out loud exclaiming, "I forgot about that."

"Jesus H. Christ," said his friend, "This place looks like a bomb went off."

"A bomb did go off," shouted Santa..."In my shorts it went off. It was a two on the Richter scale. I'm still enjoying the after shock."

Moose, in red Long John's, takes the heavy lady by the arm and says in a confidential way, "If it's free, warm and moves...Santa likes it."

The room was beginning to fill up with customers, and the people already seated wore New Year's Eve hats. Some blew their horns adding to the noise. There was a vacant table near the stage and the patrons sitting next to it were getting covered in toilet paper. As they sat there Moose and Eddie un-rolled the Scott Tissue until only the card board inserts were left. Then Eddie took the roll and using it like a Mega Phone, he announced to the room that King Shithead had arrived.

"That's what we want," said the robust man, "To sit right in front of the stage."

"The way you're built," said Moose, "You could sit both in front and back at the same time."

"Hey," said his wife, "We're lucky we got here at all. The roads were icy on Long Island."

Without hesitation Louie yells, "You came here from Long Island? Right away I could tell that you're not Jewish. Number one, no Jew is gonna ride on an icy road just to get to a joint like this, and number two, the highway's got a ten cent toll."

"Dimes a lot of money, but then again, when a Jew gets it in his head to do something, he does it."

Once again Moose takes the lady by the arm, and putting his head on her shoulder, he says, "I wish you'd get me in your head to do something."

"Don't do it, Lady. Keep your head out of his business," yells Eddie. Eddie has a short thick body and a Jerry Colonna mustache. He's funny to look at. His red striped shirt and fishing hat are topped off with a purple vest.

Fighting to get everyone's attention, Otto blows Taps on a Bugle while pointing it at Eddie's schmuck. He then stands on a chair and says, "These are nice people who deserve to be treated with respect."

Turning towards the new arrivals, he says, "Sir, don't worry about a thing. I'm going to take care of you like you were a part of my family. No matter what's happened so far, I want you to disregard anything that these uncouth bastards have said. You can count on me to cater to your every wish."

The foursome laughed at the seriousness of the waiters tone. He was wearing a black and white striped prison suit with a large fox tail hanging from his belt. The tail hung suggestively between his knees. The leader of the foursome answered, "Hey, it's no problem. We're here to have a good time and to tell you the truth, I'd love to get that table up front, and then order up a few drinks."

"The table up front is yours. I hope that makes you happy."

"Hey…that's great."

"You're happy?"

"I'm thrilled."

"Good…now tell me fat ass, what are you drinking."

That's the way I remember the night starting. *New Years Eve* at *The Crazy Country Club* is hard to explain. I'd been working there about eight months, and still the newness of it all hadn't worn thin.

Everything we did seemed funny. We dressed any way we wanted to in a room where nothing matched. Audiences filled the room week after week. I still feel that there was never another place quite like it.

I would go to work knowing that anything could happen and I loved that. As a kid I could tell jokes for hours on end. I had a reputation as a clown, a joker. When I did my bits I'd have a blast, but now, here I was, working with ten other guys just like me. Every laugh was magnified. It enriched my life. It gave me a purpose. Act crazy and get paid for it…unbelievable.

The events that led to the Clubs creation probably would have never occurred had they happened to a regular working stiff. Lucky for me, they happened to *Crazy Louie.* Let me take you back to the beginning.

Chapter 2

The Beginning

In 1948, a twenty-seven year old garment worker and a war veteran, got together to buy a bar in the Bay Ridge section of Brooklyn. The wounded veteran, George D'Amoto, had only one leg and some money that he had saved. The other man, Lou Burdo, possessed a golden personality and a gift for telling jokes, a great voice and an old guitar. He had no money.

When they first entered the bar on Ninety Second street and Seventh Avenue, they saw a few old men sitting in the back playing cards. Not much else was happening and it was no wonder. The bar was only licensed to sell beer and no one was drinking. It was depressing to say the least.

The building was a one story wooden structure that appeared to be sinking into the broken concrete that surrounded it. The creaking walls and slanted front porch only hinted as to how bad the condition of the building was. If a glass of beer was dropped there would be no fear of a puddle forming, because gravity was on the job, and it would either go through the floor, or run out the front door. The only good thing about this bar was its location.

The bar was called *The Country Club* because it was directly across the street from the *Dyker Park Golf Course*. Down the street was the *Veterans*

Hospital, which Lou and George thought would be a good source of customers. All things considered, it seemed like a good opportunity. *The Second World War* was over and everyone was scrambling to get their lives back on track. They decided to buy. George, had the money, Lou had the talent, now all they needed was customers.

After a few short weeks of cleaning and improving where they could, they managed to nudge out the old card players. One unexpected benefit that they hadn't considered was the waterfront nearby. On occasion they would get a small group of sailors from foreign countries, and more then once they were visited by sailors from Norway. Their Norwegian accent amused Louie, and he noted that they'd mentioned watching a ball game. One sailor approached him and asked in his thick accent, "Ven er yoo gonna get a telewision?" Louie was impressed. If this was the way to add customers, then he'd buy one.

After purchasing and setting up the television, the next step would be to advertise it. He set out to find an inexpensive sign maker. He contracted for a large sign to read "We Have Television" and paid the man. He left the store only to be stopped in his tracks by a thought. Always the comedian, he reentered the sign store and told the man he wanted to make a change. Louie told him that he wanted the sign to read, "We Have Telewision." The sign maker thought him crazy but did his bidding.

When the sign was delivered to the bar, he hung it in the window, not knowing what reaction to expect. People began to enter the bar just to tell him that his sign was misspelled. Louie would seize the opportunity and coax them in for a ten cent beer and surprise them with a song and a joke. The ten cent beers began to add up. So did the work load, which proved to be too much for George D'Amoto. Trying to keep up on one leg became increasingly difficult for him. George decided to beg out of the business. He offered Lou a great deal, in that he only wanted what he had invested and would accept fifty dollars a week as payment. Lou would always think well of George D'Amoto.

One afternoon a man entered the bar and sat down. He seemed troubled and Louie saw that he carried an army helmet under his arm. He ordered a beer and Lou engaged him in light conversation. Asked what was wrong, the man remarked as he held up his helmet, "I carried my helmet all through the war, and I always thought it would bring me good luck, so I kept it after I was discharged. The man went on to explain that his wife had been complaining lately about his war memorabilia and that there was no room for it in their small apartment. Feeling terrible, and not able to throw away his helmet, he had been out walking the streets. Suddenly, his eyes brightened as he said to Louie, "Hey, would you want it?"

Louie, without hesitation, replied,"Sure. I'll put it right up here on the wall so that when you come in for a beer, you can see it. Okay?"

The man was so relieved that he gave Louie the helmet and had another beer to celebrate. He swore that he'd be back.

Shortly after that, men who had memorabilia from their own war years began to show up. They'd have a beer and hang their stuff on the walls. Word began to spread as the walls of the club began to sport all kinds of military uniforms. Encouraged by Louie, the veterans felt relieved to have this outlet at their disposal. Not only did the people like it, but it spurred conversation, and that sold more beer. Something good was happening. The Club was taking on a new life. Louie realized that he had hit upon something that was being embraced by the people, and he had to keep it going.

Not having the money to buy things to hang, he decided to take a ride to the City Dump. While rummaging through the mountains of garbage, he came across a large box that was still sealed. He dragged the box out of the heap and upon opening it he found it full of ladies hats. He quickly loaded the box of manufacturer's defective hats into his car and went back to the Club. It seemed that anything that you could hang on the walls became a conversation piece. Once again he saw his business increase.

The feedback he got from the people was that they liked the idea of an inexpensive neighborhood bar where they could go and relax and hear a joke or two.

The truth was that you never got bored at the Club because Louie was always fooling around. He'd think nothing of Jumping on the bar and doing a song, and his laugh was infectious. Laughter brought more laughter. Couples began to show up at night just to have a beer and hear a tune. The Club had a warm feel to it. No one stayed a stranger for long. Louie had begun to play guitar at the age of ten. Always the crowd pleaser, it appeared that his early years would prove to serve him well.

Chapter 3

Making a name

The Club was fast becoming a popular night spot. Many of the patrons wanted to know why only beer was being served. They suggested that Louie get a liquor license so that whiskey and mixed drinks could be available. It certainly made sense that the better the variety, the happier the customer. That fell in line with the crowds staying longer and consuming more. The problem, was, that in New York State, a liquor license was only given to establishments that served both liquor and food.

Louie did some checking and found that one of the ways *The New York State Liquor Authority* checked on a bar's selling food, was to view their gas bill. The logic was that if gas was being used, the bar must be cooking. He came up with a plan.

He decided to reconnect the gas line to the old stove in the back room, and just let it burn. He did this for weeks without doing any cooking, and then reapplied for the license. After a short wait, the license was granted. With one simple move he satisfied both The State Liquor Authority and his customers.

A bar without food didn't seem to bother anyone, but one day in 1951 he was thinking about putting an ad in the New York City phone book. So far Louie had done no advertising. His thinking was that an ad could bring in more customers. As he pondered the fact that he had a Bar and Grill with no food, he said out loud, "That's lousy."

Always seeing the comical side of a situation, he thought to himself, "That's it. I'll just give them lousy food and warm beer."

The idea was a good one because the Club was all about fun and crazy times, from the walls and ceiling that sported all sorts of objects, to the personality of the men who worked there. He decided to advertise as Warm Beer and Lousy Food.

When he made the call to the phone company and gave his request, they immediately balked. They flatly stated that they would not run an ad with the word lousy in it. Louie thought quickly and said, "What if we use the word lumpy?"

Again they refused the ad. Again Louie countered in desperation.

"What if we use the word, loosely food?"

Again they refused. Not knowing what else to do, he went with the Clubs original name with just a slight twist and suggested, *The Crazy Country Club.* He was surprised when they agreed. Still, he loved the idea of the slogan he'd come up with, so once again he was off to his friend the sign maker.

An enormous sign was made and hung on the front of the bar, which proved to be a great advertisement in its own right. The phrase alone gave you an indication of what to expect inside. Between the veterans and the hospital staff, the walls were now covered with skeletons wearing army uniforms and the like. Bed pans, plastic arms and legs hung everywhere. Street signs hung everywhere. Toilet paper for napkins stood on the bar.

Once again, Louie summoned the sign maker. He'd decided that he wanted to place jokes on the walls so that anywhere you looked you'd get a laugh. The sturdy black cardboard signs were made and nailed to the walls. I still recall the first one that caught my eye. It read, "Did you hear about the female astronaut who got pregnant? It seems she was hit with a guided muscle."

Now that may not fracture your funny bone, but after a few drinks and reading about fifty of them, you'd find yourself laughing. Now add to that, the wit of the bartenders who could add to the jokes and personalize the material, and it worked. Throw in a few songs and the night was complete, with drinking, music and laughs. All of this for a few bucks was hard to beat.

As the business grew so did the work. Louie needed help. He had a keen sense of what was required to work at the Club. First, they'd have to be in need of a weekend job. Second, they'd have to be ready and able to wear many hats, comfortable with doing whatever was needed. He needed punctual and reliable men who could be counted on to be there week after week, and go from singing a song to mopping the floors at night. That was all part of the gig. Most important was that he wanted guys who saw the funny side of life. Of course, if you could sing and tell a good joke, that was even better. The key personality trait that we all shared was humor. Disagreements were far and few between. If there was any drama, it came from the challenge of not letting anyone out quip you. You had to be funnier, quicker and crazier then they were. If you needed help, there would always be someone there to do whatever was required in order to get you a laugh. It's important to understand that every waiter had his own individual mini-show going on all night at his tables. This had nothing to do with the stage show except to set the guidelines of what might happen. People would forewarn their friends, that they better be able to take a joke, because these guys were crazy. Here's an example.

One night, the place was packed, and Larry was working the opposite side of the room from me. He moved quickly for a big guy and possessed a strong powerful voice. He had a table of two couples who, it seemed, were up for anything. One of the girls was extremely pretty. The braless beauty wore a tight fitting tee shirt with horizontal stripes that molded her breasts perfectly. Larry was yelling so loud that I couldn't ignore him even though I was running to keep up with the workload. I sensed that he had a little show going on that included the interest of all the people around the table in question. I ran to his table and sounding very serious, I said, "Quick, I'm very busy. I got my own pain-in-the-asses to worry about. What do you want?"

Larry looked at me and said, "Her boyfriend wants me to count all her stripes, and I'm having trouble with my numbers. I can't seem to complete the count."

Then turning towards the girl he put out his pointing finger and began poking and counting the stripes on her chest. The tables around her began to laugh. She showed no fear at being touched and in fact, thrust her bosom forward. When he got to what proved to be her nipple area, he turned to me and with a quizzical look, he said, "What comes after four?"

Without flinching or smiling or showing any emotion at all, I said, "Five," as I poked her in the nipple. The girl looked incredulous as I turned and ran saying I was too busy to hang out. Larry looked like a light bulb had gone on as he said, "Five. That's it. Thanks". Then he simply turned and went back to work. The tables around her screamed in laughter and her boyfriend said, "I told you they were crazy."

That's an extreme example of what we could do, and get away with, primarily because the only thing we were shooting for was laughs. Nobody felt threatened and I'm sure Larry did his job by working his way up to this point through conversation. You had to know what you were doing and who you were doing it to. If you had an ulterior motive behind your actions, believe me, the people would know it. Some enjoyed participating more than others. You had to have a keen sense of these things. You needed to be a people's person. Common sense ruled. Louie used to preach, "There's two ways to say shit. One way may be disgusting while the other might be funny. It's all in the delivery. Make sure you're always funny. Remember, there are people here old enough to be your mother. They're here and they're ready to laugh, so abuse them in a funny way. Don't piss anyone off."

I must say that I think we mastered the handling of people. If a crippled person was brought to the Club by family or friends, it was usually done because they were in need of a good laugh. They knew that we'd pay special attention to them. It didn't matter what we did, as long as we pampered them in our own unique way.

One night, a lady on a wheelchair came to the Club. Sal the doorman held the party outside as we searched for a small battery operated motor from a child's toy. It had the loud roar of a lawn mower. Outside the Club, the lady as well as her family watched and laughed as we attached the large motor and flags to her wheelchair. Then with a burst of energy, through the door we pushed her. The woman was hysterical with laughter as the motor roared and the horns blew as we propelled her around and through the Club.

There were moments when her wheelchair almost flipped but rather then showing fear, she just laughed that much harder. At the end of the night her family was quick to thank us and say that she really needed the laughs, and that we were the best medicine she'd received in a long time. That was the kind of thing that topped even a nice tip.

Whatever walked in the room was fair game. If you were short or tall, skinny or fat, you were a target. What balanced things off was when someone absolutely beautiful walked in feeling all good and a bit cocky about their appearance. The tables would turn quickly as one of us would say, "What are you doing here? Are you trying to make us ugly bastards feel bad? Why don't you and Miss Perfect take a walk to a bar that caters to mannequins? I think there's one in Ohio."

There's nothing that leveled the playing field more then, knowing that no one was untouchable. ·

The Fort Hamilton Army Base was also near the Club, and soldiers being boys, were always on the prowl for girls. They knew a girl willing to go to the Club would probably have a good sense of humor. On many occasions I'd have a soldier say to me, "Listen, this is our first date. I don't know how far this girl will go, so would you do a favor and ask her if she puts out?"

Everybody wanted to be a comedian, but didn't know how. Now, obviously, this guy is a bit of a jerk, so we'd turn the tables on him by first whispering in the girl's ear and then fake listening to her reply. Turning to the guy we'd announce to him and anyone who could hear us, "Well, sure, she'll put out…but not for you… you sorry son of a bitch."

Then, leaning close to the guy, we'd say, "Schmuck. You'd have had a better chance if you had taken her to a nice restaurant. Why'd you take her to this shit hole anyway?"

So now we had saved the girl, and insulted the guy as well as our own Club. How could anybody get mad at us for insulting our own Club? Fair was fair. You couldn't expect to sit there laughing at everyone else and not laugh at yourself when it was your turn. Everybody got their turn at the Country Club.

In August of 1954, a reporter from *The New York Daily News* came to the Club and did a story on it. It featured two large photos of the Club, one showing a bartender taking a bottle of booze from a trap door in the ceiling, and another of a lady getting a monkey dropped from the ceiling onto her head. The article appeared as, *"Hijinks are on the house."* It read, "The bartender suddenly whipped out a gun and stared coldly at the man across the bar. Helpless, the victim threw up his hands in supplication, but the villain's cruel smile promised no mercy. His fingers slowly squeezed the trigger and phf-f-f-t. Amidst a roar of laughter the murdered man sheepishly wiped the water from his face, another victim of the endless pranks pulled at *The Country Club Bar and Grill, 9032 Seventh Avenue, Brooklyn.*"

The article then went on to tell how Louie had started his business and how loyal the patrons were. Truth be told, many of his patrons were repeat business bringing friends in to be entertained and to show off the place as if it were their own. There was a sense of a partnership associated with the Club that said to the rest of the city, "Look what we have. There isn't another one like it in the entire world, and yet, we have it right here in Brooklyn."

The patrons also had their favorite waiters and a feeling of intimacy between many of them existed. It felt great to give a table all you had, and I always felt it a compliment if when they left, they seemed a little befuddled by the night's experience. Many times you'd hear things like, "Next week I'm bringing my cousin Patty. He's one cheap bastard and he wears a wig. Give it to him good, okay?"

Now all we had to do was hone up on wig jokes and give it good to Patty. That solidified our patrons because we did their bidding, and gave Patty the opportunity to get even with someone else. It was like a snowball going downhill. We couldn't lose.

Chapter 4

The Big Secret

Doesn't it seem unlikely that anyone born and raised in Brooklyn New York, a city unto itself that is alive with the media and news, would never hear of such an outrageous night spot as *The Crazy Country Club?* Well, not only was I in that category, but so was my entire family, and friends, too. Maybe it was the Clubs lack of advertising that did it. I'll never know. The first time I heard about the Club, I was in California, and strange as it may seem, I learned of it from my mother.

I was stationed out west from 1959 to 1963. Like all the servicemen of that era, I depended on letters from home to keep in touch. Mail was important in those days. There was no e-mail, and phone calls were too expensive for an enlisted man.

My mother was a terrific letter writer, and I always looked forward to mail call. She had a wonderful sense of humor and the ability to put it on paper. In our home, my father did all the singing and my mother told the jokes. I am blessed by having some of each of their talents. I sang like my father and told jokes like my mother. It was only fitting that I do something with them. The reason I bring this up is because of an incident that happened years later at a friend's house party.

There were about thirty or forty people at this party and without my realizing it, my hosts placed all the chairs into a theatre setting. I was then asked to get up and tell some jokes.

After doing the half hour I was approached by an older couple. The man spoke to me first. He said, "By chance, is your mother's name Virginia?"

Not knowing the couple, I was surprised to hear they knew my mother's name, and thought maybe a practical joke was in the making. He continued, "As you were telling jokes I could see your mother up there. Her name is Virginia, right?"

I answered yes as he said "And your fathers name is John. I remember him singing, and playing the Guitar."

Well, there you go. I found it uplifting to hear those words especially since I knew them to be true. Every letter I ever received from my mother always had a tinge of humor in it. To her, funny was important. It helped get you through the day.

When mail call came that day in 1962, I had no knowledge of the Country Club. My mother began in her usual way, filling me in about my family. Then she made mention of a recent night out they'd had. My Mom was very close with her siblings, and they often went out socially together. My uncle Nick had been working on 64th Street and went to the Club for coffee and lunch. Knowing the kind of man that Louie was, and knowing about his operation, he set up a date to go there with some of the family. He wouldn't say much about the club except to say that it was a lot of fun. He knew they'd like it.

Mom started out by saying that when they arrived at the Club, she just couldn't believe her eyes. The building was completely painted pink with large black polka dots all over it. She wrote that there was a long line of people waiting to get in and that every few minutes, men from inside the Club would emerge dressed in prison uniforms and the like, just to abuse those on line. As these men escorted patrons into the Club, laughter and bugles being blown could be heard from within.

When it was their turn to be seated, the door man yelled out that he had a table of twelve. As he said, "Twelve more pain in the asses", the waiters converged on them, yelling and blowing kazoos. From inside you could hear people laughing, bells ringing and horns blowing. As my aunt Marianne entered the Club, popcorn dropped down on her head, pretty much covering her. It was madness. Mom wrote that the inside of this Club was hard to explain. The walls and ceiling were plastered with objects that would take forever to see and read. The waiters were yelling for their party to follow them, and so the procession began. Round and a round they went, up one aisle and down the next, going in circles all the way. They found themselves in the back of the Club. There were three doors; two for the restroom and another door which led to an alley way.

Without warning, a waiter took my mother by the arm as another waiter opened the alley door. With one swift move they pushed her out into the alley, and locked the door. Mom said she heard the waiters say as they were pushing her, "Stay out, you bastard. We've only got room for eleven."

When my mom stopped laughing, she made her way out of the alley and approached the line she'd just been on. A waiter met her and continued the abuse.

"Jesus," he said aloud, "Everybody was okay with the instructions on how to sit down except her. We get at least one dumb bastard a night and I guess that she's it." Everyone on line was laughing as the waiter continued.

"Her husband told me to leave her in the alley. That's where he first met her anyway."

The waiter then smiled and said to the group, "I'm only kidding. Maybe the mix up was partly our fault. If we would have told her to lie down she probably would have gotten it right the first time."

He then turned to my mother and said, "Please lady, don't embarrass me a second time. This time when I point to a seat, don't introduce yourself to it, just sit down on the son of a bitch. Okay?"

She went on to write that the fun continued all night long as the waiters sang songs, and told jokes. That was the first time I heard of the Club. The location they went to was on Seventh Avenue and 64th Street. It didn't ring a bell when I was reading my Moms letter that I had actually been to the original Club on 92nd Street a year and a half earlier.

What happened was that after basic training was over I was given military leave for eighteen days. My best friend, Larry, had mentioned this crazy bar he'd heard of. One afternoon we decided to take a ride and check it out. The bar was quiet that afternoon, with only a handful of patrons. We looked around and had a beer and left. We had dates that night so we decided to return with the girls.

The transformation that took place from day to night was unbelievable. The street was now crowded with traffic. There was a doorman outside the Club dressed in an Army uniform. His coat and hat were completely covered with medals. He carried a

slapping stick, which is made by connecting two boards on one end by a hinge. The bottom board has a small needle protruding through a hole in the top board. When slapped with the stick, the two boards would come together with a loud smacking noise. It would sting a little if it hit you, but more then that it was the apprehension of getting whacked that caused nervous laughter.

We had trouble parking and decided to leave and come back another time. Who would have thought that just a few years later we would both be working for Louie.

There was one other occasion when the club was mentioned. After being discharged from the Air Force, I was honored to be asked to stand up for a friend from Worcester Massachusetts. One of the men in the bridal party had been stationed at Fort Hamilton Army Base, and he loved to hear jokes. He couldn't understand how I'd never heard of the Crazy Country Club, being that I was from Brooklyn. It was ironic to me that he'd said to me on many occasions that he thought I should be working at the club. What a small world we live in.

Those were the only times I'd heard of the Club. Mom's description was more informative, than even my own trip there. I put it on my list of things to do and basically forgot about it.

One day I received a call from my uncle Nick. He told me that his friend was looking for a full time bartender. He told Louie that I was available and I'd done some singing in the Air Force. Lou agreed to see me and a date was set for us to meet at the Club. You would think that I would have had a good idea of what to expect after all that I'd been told about the Club. Nothing could be further from the truth.

Chapter 5

Eddie, and Rolly-Polly

In 1962, forced to leave the building on ninety second street, Louie decided to build his own club. He purchased a corner lot on 64th Street and began construction. Although he subcontracted, he and his father both worked on the job. The building was designed so that it could accommodate both his bar and a rental unit in order to defray his operating cost. He rented it to an auto body shop run by a big man named Dominick. I tell you this in order to explain how Louie met Eddie.

Eddie drove a truck and delivered auto parts. He was completing a delivery one day to Dominick's shop when he heard the sound of hammering. As curious as a child, he followed the sounds into Louie's bar. As Eddie entered the bar, his eyes quickly scanned the bar, and the more he saw the more he chuckled.

"What is this place," he asked?

Louie began to explain what the bar was all about as he hung signs on the wall. Eddie was fascinated. Every time he came across a new gadget he'd laugh. It seemed to Louie that there was even something comical about Eddie's body. He was short and stocky, with an ever present five o'clock shadow. He wore a pancake hat along with his work cloths, and kept a cheap cigar in his mouth. Louie guessed they were about the same age and immediately liked him.

I must interject, that both of these men had lived through the depression, and then the Second World War, so they knew the value of the buck. Something for free was never passed up. Also, they had been raised in an era where if you wanted music, you made music. Many homes, no matter how poor, had pianos and musical instruments.

As Eddie was dropping a fake spider from the ceiling to the table top below, he said, "Do you need any more stuff?"

Without much thought, Louie blurted out, "Yeah. I could use a piano."

Eddie replied, "Okay, I'll get you one. I don't know when, but I'll get you one."

When Eddie drove off Louie would have sworn that he'd seen the last of him. It was not to be so.

Three days later Louie was in the Club doing his sign hanging when an excited wide eyed Eddie showed up.

"Come on," he said. "I got you a piano and it's free. All we gotta do is remove it from his house, and it's all yours."

Louie laughed and told him, "Are you kidding me? I don't have a truck to move a piano."

Eddie countered with, "Come on, it's free. I got my truck outside. Let's go get it."

Louie thought to him self, free is free. He had nothing to lose. He closed the bar and jumped in Eddie's small delivery truck. Off they went, two strangers on a mission.

When they arrived at the house they had a rude awakening. Rather then the piano being in the front living room, it was tucked away in the furthest corner of the basement. Louie said that it looked as though the basement had been built around the piano. They decided that the only way to accomplish their task was to partly dismantle it. They did this and then somehow shoved and carried the piano up the cellar stairs and into the truck. They reached the Club and then once again wrestled with the upright. They positioned it and assembled it, and presto, *the Crazy Country Club* had a piano.

Eddie had supplied the truck and his muscle to help Louie, even though he wasn't family or friend. He asked for no compensation, and

Louie offered none. The only question that Eddie had was, "Do you need any guys to work in this Club?"

Louie took a sip from his ever present cup of black coffee, and asked, "What can you do?"

Eddie replied, "I can tell a joke," and began to sing, *"If you were the only girl in the world, and I was the only boy....I'd play with myself."*

Louie shook his head at the bad joke, but in spite of himself he began to laugh. He realized that Eddie was one of those special people you rarely run across. His timing was imperfect, but his face had many looks. In the short time that he'd known Eddie, he'd seen his face light up like a Christmas tree, look dumfounded, confused and child like with enthusiasm. He realized that Eddie was a clown. He was comical and likeable. This combination was something that you couldn't buy or teach. Add the little boy qualities that he possessed, and the amazement that he found in every day life, and you were faced with a very funny man. Louie hired him as a waiter and shortly afterwards put him into the show.

Louie's instincts had been right about Eddie. Eddie would do anything for a laugh. He learned a song that became his signature piece. The song was "Rolly Polly", and in it, Eddie would come from back stage dressed in a sheer red cape. He wore high combat boots, and red bra and panties. In both his bra and panties he had hidden different objects that he would remove during the song. In his bra he had a falsey loaded with a water squirt ball, and when called for in the song, he'd take dead aim and get some guy in the face.

In his panties he had cherries, a banana, a wig and whatever else he could stuff in there. With each stanza a new toy would be shown. Of course he had a cigar in his mouth which, more then once, almost set his blonde wig on fire. His love of gadgets and anything physical became a passion of his, and he would travel to great lengths to obtain them. I believe that every show we did had Eddie doing something physical. If he wasn't squirting water across the room, he was lighting flash paper, or making fart sounds. He really had to be watched rather than heard. Louie would sometimes get pissed if Eddie flubbed a line in a set routine, but it always seemed to work itself out. It many times ended up funnier then it was intended to be. He was a big part of the show.

The club was doing well, but Louie was still looking to increase his revenue. He thought about his ten cent beers and how they could help him at just a slightly higher price. He knew his customers. They were blue collar workers who demanded the biggest bang for their buck. He would have to justify any changes in the Club's prices. Then it hit him.

Glancing at the corner of the room, he settled on the piano. If he provided piano music to dance with and sing along with, he could get an increase. He took out an ad seeking an experienced pianist. Within a short time he received a response. The gentlemen, was a soft spoken man, who informed Louie that he had actually played piano for The Horn and Hardart Talent Show. They agreed on fifteen dollars a night. The man would play from nine o'clock to midnight. He would start on Friday.

The way Louie figured it, if he made the beers fifteen cents and sold three hundred a night, it would cover the cost of the pianist. The rest would be a profit. He liked his plan, but as they say in the bar business, you never know what the night will bring.

Normally, on a Friday night, the waiters would come in to work at about eight o'clock. It didn't take long to set up. The tables were already cleaned. Laying down empty tuna fish cans for ashtrays was easy. People would start showing up around eight-thirty, and by nine-thirty the place would be at capacity. Usually, the show would go on around ten O'clock. That's what Louie figured would happen on the pianist' first night.

Well, think again.

At eight o'clock the door opened and a man walked in. He was wearing sunglasses and using a cane to maneuver. Louie thought to himself, this is a first. The first customer of the night, and he happens to be blind. It must be another veteran that heard of the place. Louie approached the man from behind the bar and asked, "How can I help you, Pal? Would you like a beer?"

The blind man turned in Lou's direction and said, "I'd like to see Lou Burdo."

"I'm Lou Burdo. What can I do for you?"

The man said, "I'm Ralph, and I'm here to play piano for you."

Lou was taken back for a moment. The man continued as if he knew what Lou was thinking, "Oh, don't worry about me being blind. I've been playing for years and I'm really quite good. Should I start playing now?"

"No," Lou yelled, "Not now. There's no one here. You just sit at the bar and have a drink. I'll tell you when to start."

Well, nine turned to ten, and ten o'clock to eleven o'clock, and still the only ones in the Club was Louie, his crew and the blind man.

Suddenly, as if by magic, the door opened and people began coming in. There were groups of six, and of ten, some came as couples and as singles. Within twenty minuets the place was full. Louie ran to Blind Ralph and, taking him by his arm, led him to the piano.

"Start playing now," Louie yelled over the noise, "And don't stop until I tell you to."

It turned out that Ralph was correct when he said that he knew his way around a key board. The people began to dance and sing along. Some inquired about the price change but when Lou explained about the live music, they accepted it. Most of them did, anyway.

In the neighborhood lived a man named John Conte. It was a well known fact that he loved his beer and was known to be a regular. When Conte ordered his first beer, he threw a quarter on the bar. When Lou served him he tossed him a dime's change. Conte failed to get Lou's attention, but eventually caught him by the arm as he passed by.

"Hey Lou," he said. "I think you made a mistake with my change. You only gave me a dime back."

Lou took a deep breath and explained.

"You know John, now that we have piano music the beers have gone up from ten cents to fifteen cents. We're just like the other night clubs now."

Conte looked at Lou, and already a little drunk, he said nothing. Seeing Conte trying to digest this new information, Lou moved off. A half hour later the place was in full swing. The blind man was banging away at the keyboard, the people were dancing and every bar stool and table was full. The Club's noise level was at a new high. Louie was thrilled.

Suddenly and without any warning, John Conte, the neighborhood drunk, stood up on top of his bar stool, and screamed. Louie, thinking that there must be something medically wrong with the man, screamed back at him, "What's wrong John, what's wrong?"

You could hear a pin drop as Conte looked around the quieted room and very seriously said, "Quick Louie, quick. Give me one of those ten cent beers before the fucking music starts playing again."

Louie laughed out loud as he looked around and said, "Only here, can this shit happen. Only here."

Chapter 6

Meeting The Boss

My first meeting with Louie was in April of 1965. My uncle had set up the interview for a Friday afternoon and I was anxious to meet him. I needed a job. I drove my 1957' Thunderbird the few miles from home to the Club and found a parking spot. The weather was mild and as I approached the Seventh Avenue entrance to the Club, I could see that the door was propped open for some fresh air. The familiar aroma of Italian cooking hit me as I knocked on the open door and called out. A voice from inside told me to come in. That's when I got my first look at the guy my family had so talked about. Between my mothers bragging about his jokes, to my fathers comments about how well he could sing and play guitar, I was expecting a giant. It was not so.

As I entered the kitchen he was bent over a stove pulling a large tray from the oven. The bald man was shirtless and had an unlit cigar clamped in his teeth. He wore dark rimmed glasses, and when he stood to move the tray of food to the counter, I noticed his barrel chest.

Standing five foot seven with squared shoulders and thick neck, he appeared to be powerful. With a large spatula he moved the dozens of meatballs that crowded the tray, turning them for an even cook. He lifted and slid the tray back into the oven. Then, standing, he said through clenched teeth, "Are you Nick's nephew?"

I walked in with my hand extended and introduced myself. He wiped his hands on his apron and shook mine. I thought to myself that I had just met the cook. I could see what he was making but asked him anyway. He said, "Balls. Everybody loves my balls. I'm Louie." He laughed quietly as his shoulders shook. His eyes watched me, looking for my reaction. I laughed.

He poured us a cup of coffee. The coffee pot stood out because I'd only seen a pot that size at my mother's house. It was probably big enough to perk twenty cups, however, all that my mother used hers for, was lemonade. Her pot was always Brillo'd shiny. Lou's pot looked discolored and dirty to me. Once, when my brother Andy was working in the kitchen, he got a talking to from Louie for washing it. "Never wash this pot," Louie yelled. "You'll kill the taste."

He showed me the Bar and explained the job. It was six days a week, Monday through Thursday from six to midnight, Friday and Saturday from eight to closing. The pay was ninety dollars a week plus tips. I told him I had no experience tending bar but nothing seemed to faze him. He replied, "Can you pop a top on a beer bottle?"

I assured him I could, "But what about mixed drinks," I asked?

He reached behind the bar and retrieved a small red book. "This book," he said, "Has every drink you've ever heard of. If someone asks you for a fancy drink, just look it up. Tell him a joke while he's waiting, and have a good time, gabesh?"

We shook on the deal, and I was excited. Louie told me to get my cabaret license. The truth was, I had nothing going for me. I was uneducated and without a trade. My four years in the Air Force had proved fruitless. Except for my time in a troupe doing shows, I had learned little. In short, I was a singing truck driver.

I wanted to make a decent appearance, so I went shopping for a new shirt. Thirteenth Avenue in Boro Park, had the best clothing stores, and the first store I walked into I caught a real break. The shirt I liked was the last one of its kind, the bearded man assured me, and on sale. I bought it for two dollars. Now I was ready for work.

My first night was one for the books. After opening the bar I settled into the routine that Louie had proposed. There were no customers so I began by removing the whiskey bottles from the shelf one row at a time, and cleaning them. Louie had stressed that the club did very little business on week days. However, there was a small group of regulars that would show up. He stayed open more for deliveries and advertising then anything else.

By ten o'clock there were a few guys from the junk yard and a few neighborhood girls. All together, there were about ten people drinking, mostly beer. At this point in time the only worker I had met at the Club was Louie, so when the door opened and in came this bubbly little guy, I didn't know what to make of it.

"Hey," he asked? "Are you John? I'm Eddie. I work here as a waiter and do the shows with Louie."

He had a big grin on his face and a slight stutter to his chuckle. He walked behind the bar and took me by the arm.

"Have you been in the ladies room yet?" Pulling on my arm, he said, "Come on, I'll show you."

Some of the regulars began to laugh at the surprised look on my face as Eddie led me down the aisle towards the ladies room. I didn't know what to expect. When I told him that a girl was in the restroom he said "That's okay, we're not gonna bother her. We just want the door."

To my surprise he reached in and opened the door just enough to get a grip on it. Then he lifted. Presto, the door was free in his hands. The girl screamed as he started walking towards the bar carrying the door. He remarked as he walked, "I'll just leave the door here," as he propped the door against the bar. The girl in the bathroom had a friend who ran to the ladies room to aid her. In a moment they both emerged laughing, not believing that something like that could happen. They weren't angry but instead talked wide-eyed about the experience, with one asking, "What were you doing in there," and the other answering, "I was only washing my hands."

Eddie said out loud, "She was washing something, all right…I think we better leave it like that."

Eddie then explained, "That's what we do when they go during a show." It turned out that he had watched the girl enter the ladies room. He knew she wouldn't have enough time to get into an embarrassing position. Frequently, a young girl would get up during the show thinking that she'd just quietly make her way to the ladies room. Of course she'd be spotted by Louie on stage, just waiting for this to happen.

Louie would stop speaking and just stare at the girl as she walked by and say to Eddie, "Where's she going?"

Eddie would answer that he didn't know. Louie would then say quietly, "Excuse me Miss. Oh, Miss, excuse me. Where are you going? Don't you know that during the show you're not supposed to go to the ladies room."

Now everyone on stage would start asking the same question with the waiters adding to the frenzy of the inquisition, saying, "Stop that girl. She can't take it upon her self, and interrupt the show just because she can't hold her water…stop that girl."

The girls would always react in the same way. As she quickened her step towards the ladies room looking for sanctuary, she'd appear apprehensive. Making her way into the bathroom, she'd look back at the stage as if to say, "See, I made it."   In addition to that, you could feel some relief from all the ladies in the room, because what could happen to her, might happen to them.

By that time, the waiters would be right behind her. Instead of stopping at the door, they'd all file into the bathroom. After a few moments and some screaming, they'd do exactly what Eddie had shown me, and remove the door. Now with the audience laughing and the girl screaming, the waiters would carry the door as they yelled for the doorman. Sal would appear saying, "You called for a doorman," and they'd say, "Are you the doorman?" Sal would answer, "Sure I'm the doorman," and the waiters would say, "Good. Here's a door."

That was it. The bit never failed. The girls in question were no worse for their troubles, and the bit varied little. It turned out if a girl was in dire need of the ladies room, they'd go to it three at a time, posting a lookout at the door. I never saw a bad reaction to that bit.

After Eddie left, the night was uneventful until two men entered the bar dressed in suits. My impression was that they might be mob connected guys. They were quiet in their manner, and ordered beer and shots. Taking two stools at the end of the bar, they went into a quiet conversation.

As I began washing glasses a young guy caught my attention. He was having words with one of the girls, and as I looked up I saw the girl reach back and smack the guy in the face. It was a forceful blow and the guy instinctively reached back and hit the girl.

Without thinking, my right foot went onto the sink's edge and over the bar I went, grabbing the guy by the neck and tossing him. We both went flying to the floor. He got up and put his hands up to fight but as I went towards him he backed out of the bar.

What happened next was that two of the men from the junkyard offered to follow and beat the shit out of him. I told them it wasn't necessary. It seemed that I had made a few friends for having defended the girl.

The other thing that amazed me was that the two men in suits were not connected guys like I thought. They were cops. One was the Captain of the local precinct and the other, one of his detectives. They relayed the story to Louie, who asked them what he should do about it. They said the reason they didn't get involved was because it was over before it begun. Louie asked them if there was anything that he should do. The Captain smiled and answered," Whatever you do, don't fuck with the bartender." They told him I handled it well, and not to worry. The worst part of my first night was that during the scuffle, I had ripped my new two dollar shirt. My first night turned out to be some bargain, with my tips not even covering the cost of the shirt.

Chapter 7

Parade Day

New York City is indeed the melting pot of America, with every neighborhood hosting a variety of cultures. Most areas, although fully integrated, are still dominated by one group or another. In Windsor Terrace, where I grew up, the Italians and Irish were greatest in numbers. There were churches everywhere to affirm that. Nearby in Boro Park, there was a large concentration of Jewish people. Most of the homes and businesses there were owned by them. And so it went. If someone was to ask me where all the Norwegian's lived, I would have been at a loss to tell them, although everyone seemed to know someone named Olsen. It turned out that there was a large community of Norwegians in Bay Ridge and Sunset Park. The Club sat right in the middle of those two neighborhoods.

Once a year the Norwegians celebrated by having a parade. The event was something to see, with bands playing, children marching, and a truckload of beautiful blondes and redheads smiling and waving. The street was always crowded with proud onlookers waving their flags. That's the way it went until the sun went down.

When darkness fell, the mothers would take their kids and tuck them in bed, sit back and take a well deserved break. A funny thing happened to the men. They usually started drinking during the day and would be quite drunk by nightfall. Their idea of a good time was to close every bar that they could stagger into. The number of bars in Bay Ridge was astounding. It's unreasonable to think, that you could drink and close down every one of them, but when you're drunk, anything seems possible. As the years passed a solution was found. They would go to a bar and have a few drinks, then start a fight, destroying the room. That would surely force the bar to close. Then they could move on to the next one. Now, that's an ingenious plan, don't you think? Well, not if you're the one tending bar, it isn't.

Louie had mentioned that when he first opened his place, a group of young toughs had paid him a visit and informed him that they were going to be running things at the Club. That was when Louie first started "Couples only night." That kept the roaming gangs away. Their interest was in drinking and fighting. If there was no one to do battle with, they wanted no part of it. As time passed, he eased up on that rule, and allowed singles to enter. Eventually the Club became a favorite spot for bachelor parties. So it became known that Norwegian Day was the worst day to be working a bar, and there I was, about to be baptized under fire.

My first experience with them occurred as darkness fell on my first Parade night. There wasn't a soul in the Club. I was behind the bar wiping bottles when they entered. There were six of them. They were all blonde headed guys who were dressed in dark suits. They wore white shirts and ties, and until I got a better look, they appeared to be quite professional. Then I took a closer look. What I saw I didn't like.

Their jackets and shirts were crumpled and twisted as if someone had man-handled them. Some of their shirts were ripped and all of their ties hung loosely about their necks. Some of them showed a bruise or swollen lip. I checked for my bat under the counter as I watched them stagger to the bar. They came to an abrupt halt and wavered as they tried to stand tall. Since working at the Club, I had to on many occasions use my wit and sense of humor to bail me out of a sticky situation with a drunk. I've found that when it comes to dealing with drunks, it's a real crap shoot. It's difficult to tell if they're going to be funny or nasty.

They ordered beers and shots of Rye. After shooting down the booze and sipping their beer, the biggest feller said, *"Ver is everybaadee?"*

I told them that when the parade ended, everyone went home. They weren't very happy to hear that there was no one left to fight, and grumbled about it to one another. I don't know why, but I thought if I told them a joke they might call it a night and not beat me to death. So I started with an old-square head story that went like this.

A wealthy Jewish man hires a beautiful blonde from Norway to work in his palatial home. Taking her on the side he tells her that he wants to help teach her some English. He says, "We have some peculiar sayings in America that may not make sense to you, so pay attention. For instance, if I'm in the mood for sex, I'll say to you that I might come downstairs later and make a sandwich. When you hear that, be ready for me. When my wife falls asleep, I'll come down to the maid's quarters to make love to you. Do you understand?"

She understands, she told him, and indeed, upon hearing the man of the house, who just before retiring, announced, "I'm getting a little hungry. Later tonight, I might come down to make a sandwich," she reacted.

The young beautiful blonde runs to her bedroom and prepares herself. She puts on her flimsiest nightgown, and lies on her bed. Suddenly, the old man bursts into her room and smothers her body with his. He moans as he buries himself into her. Looking deeply into her eyes, he asks, "Tell me sweetheart, when the boys in Norway make love, do they also call it making a sandwich?"

"Vel, ya, de do call it a sanvich ven dey make love. Only, in Norvay, when da boys make a sandwich, they put in a lot more meat."

Now, I thought that was a cute joke. Their reaction was dead silence. Their eyes showed not even a glimmer of a connection to my joke. There was nothing going on in their drunken minds. They appeared to be unsure as to whether I had insulted them or not. Still, not a word was spoken as they sipped their beer. I feared for the worst. Suddenly, the big guy staggered back and with his hands on his hips, took a long look at the walls and ceiling.

He then gathered his buddies together and whispered loud enough to be heard down the block, "Vy don ve go to a nudder bar. *It looks like somevons all ready wrecked this place."*

I called Louie and told him what had taken place and he told me to close the Club. It turned out most of the bars in Bay Ridge would close by ten o'clock on Norwegian Day because of the fighting. I bolted the doors and turned off the lights. I was safe for another year.

Chapter 8

Balls For The Queen

When I joined the Club, the crew was going through a transition period. Not everyone worked the full weekend as I did. Unlike an average weekend job, longevity was common place. No one looked any sorrier for it, and the level of energy never diminished.

Moose was there the longest, with Cappy and Otto close behind. They'd all began at the ninety second street location, witnessing the growth of the Club first hand. They were all funny guys in their own way. Moose always reminded me of Harpo Marx. I'm not sure why, but I believe it was his expressions and the way his lower lip hung. It made him appear dopey and nonchalant in his manner. In reality, he was a college-educated man who did very well for himself. He was anything but stupid. I believe the reason he worked the Club on weekends was because he loved to play the horses. He told us a story once that sounded unbelievable, but he swore it was true.

He was at a prestigious raceway down south and although uncommon for him, he hadn't laid a bet. Instead, he was in the dining room having dinner with his wife, and watching the race on television. As the horses made the turn, a large geyser of water shot up from the track. The water disrupted the horse race, throwing most of the horses into a panic. Immediately, the people in the dining room began to either rip up their tickets, or throw them into the air. Moose told his wife to stay put and just wait for him. He'd be right back.

He made his way down to the crowds of people that had gathered at the rail. As they were screaming for blood, he got on his hands and knees and began to scoop up any un-ripped tickets that he could find. He shoved them into his jacket pockets as well as down his shirt as fast as he could. The reason, he explained, was that he knew they had to declare a winner. Knowing that, he made his way to the men's room and locked himself into a stall. He then methodically sorted and made separate piles of the tickets, and waited. More then a half hour had passed when the officials made their announcement of the winner. Moose claimed that he picked up the stack of winning tickets and flushed the rest. He then went to the window and cashed in. He won twenty three hundred dollars and never had a dime on the race. He went back and found his wife a bit confused about the whole thing, so to make up for it, he took her out and bought her a new Chevy. What a character. He loved the horses so much that he eventually went and bought a home in Sarasota, New York. I once asked him why he gambled and he told me that it wasn't the winning that excited him, but just the thought that he might win. He was a great guy.

Cappy was a big man. I'm guessing he was six two and big around the middle. He was quick on his feet and carried himself well. A thick head of dark curly hair was highlighted by his thick dark rimmed glasses. He was always making remarks and smiling. He'd do anything for a laugh and the people loved him. Sometimes he'd say or sing something in English, sometimes in Italian. You could see Louie liked him a lot.

Although Cappy and I didn't work together long, he always came down the club to visit. He left the Club to go into business, and as his business grew, we saw less and less of him.

Otto was a riot, but not as a joke teller. He just liked to laugh and could be heard from a distance. The funny thing about Otto was that he liked to bitch. He'd bitch about everything, even though he'd usually end up laughing about it. He liked to refer to all the customers as hard-on's or cheap bastards. He never surprised any of us with his complaining. When the night was over, and all the customers had gone, we'd take a moment to have a drink and split up the tips. All the tips were thrown into a common pot because we did so many different jobs. Some waiters did more on the floor while others did the show. It was the fairest way. If the tips were good, Otto would comment on what a good night we'd had. If the tips weren't great, he'd move his fedora to the back of his head and the tirade would begin. He'd remember in detail, every cheap bastard that he served. The only break we'd get from his bitching was during the counting of the tips. You had to love the guy.

Lou had a large pool of men to work with. At different times there might be me, Tommy and Stevie Shades behind the bar. On the Floor you could find Otto, Moose, Eddie, Larry or Cappy. There was Johnny Nibs and Sal the doorman and over the years many others. I found that working as a bartender gave me the opportunity to employ lots of gags that I couldn't do as a waiter. Louie had special beer labels made up. They were paper thin, and when placed against a wet bottle of beer, they would stick. The label was a drawing of a horse taking a leak into a mug of beer. Under it was written, "Internally brewed". It's name, was Auspice. No one paid it any mind until the barkeep would ask, "Would you like another bottle of horse piss?"

Another gag with beer that we used was called "The singing beer." When it was requested by a customer, a bottle of Bud would be placed into a hot tub of water. Before heating the beer, a cork with a metal casing would be jammed into the bottle. The cork had many tiny openings like those of a salt shaker. Next, the waiter would put on a large glove to protect his hand. Louie would then lead the procession of waiters to the customer's table. Some of us blew into kazoos, some of us carried umbrellas. When Louie would announce that their "Singing beer," was ready, the waiter holding the beer bottle would slam it hard on the table. What happened next was both beautiful and funny.

The foam of the beer would shoot out in a perfect arch, covering an area at least five foot across. The waiters would raise their umbrellas and begin to sing, "April Showers." In a panic, everyone at the table would slide their chairs quickly away from the beer fountain, and the place would scream in laughter. It never failed that someone would come up and ask us how they could order one for their friends. We'd tell them we only did one a night. It made for a slippery floor and so a little moping was required.

Another favorite was called "Balls for the Queen." Louie's kitchen had a fast food menu like meatball or sausage hero's, shrimp on a platter, a cheese and cracker plate and burgers and French fries. When requested by a customer for a lady friend, a "Balls for the Queen," meatball sandwich would be delivered. Again, it was like a procession. When the sandwich was ready, Louie would throw on the stage lights and say over the microphone something like this.

"Ladies and gentlemen, we have a special guest in our presence tonight. If you'll direct your attention to this table over here, we're told that we have, visiting from California, Queen Lucy."

At this time Moose would move to the drums and Larry to the standup bass. The other waiters, by now, had all made it to the kitchen where they grabbed kazoos. There was also a homemade instrument that we used. It was a broom handle that was covered with bells and by striking it on the floor it would create a jingle bell sound. Eddie would use that. The bass drum and horns behind the bar were controlled by Tommy and Johnny Nibs.

Louie continued by telling the girl that we were thrilled to have royalty in the house, and even happier to be able to feed her.

"So let me say at this time, Queen Lucy, that "YOUR BALLS ARE READY.""

Otto would blow an intro on the bugle and all the waiters would then march out of the kitchen to the beat of the drum. The bugle and kazoos and bell stick would be in time with Moose's drumming, as the waiters made their way to Lucy's table and surrounded her. Louie would make his way to her table, and the waiter with the sandwich would position himself beside him. The girl by now knew that her friends had set her up. The reactions differed with everyone. Some were embarrassed by all the attention and just wanted to be done with it. Some loved it. Either way it worked.

Lou would take the sandwich, and holding it near the girl, would ask, "Are you ready for something to eat?"

The girl would confirm that she was. Lou would then begin to lower the sandwich to the table. The girl would instinctively reach for the dish. Louie would pull it back, saying, "Did you see what she did. She tried to grab my balls in mid air."

The band would play. Louie would yell, "Is that what they do in California? If they see two balls in mid air, they just grab for them? Don't let me stop you. Whatever you're comfortable with. Just, whatever you do, don't choke on this sandwich. My balls are not insured."

Louie would take his time and not rush the bit. The success of the bit much depended on the girl in question. Holding the sandwich in front of the girl, he'd ask, "Let me see how you're going to hold it. Oh, you're a two handed girl. All right, then, here's your sandwich. I hope you enjoy your meal, and remember, whenever you think of balls, please, think of us. Now, here's a bottle of champagne to wash it down with. How about a big hand for the little lady."

Then we'd go back to work. Just as quickly as it began, it would end. The stage lights would go out and all the waiters would resume their jobs like nothing had ever happened. It left all the customer's wondering what would happen next.

Chapter 9

Breaking Chops

The women that came to the Club were always a favorite target of ours. They reacted to getting any sort of attention in the form of a prank, in the same way. They screamed. Whatever we did created screams, and that was good for business.

One night as things quieted down and a group of young ladies were seated, Larry took a quarter out of his pocket, and showing it to the crowd, he threw it down to the floor, exclaiming in a booming voice, "Oops, I think I dropped my quarter."

He then dropped to the floor and began crawling under the chairs at their table, with most of us following him.

"I think I see it," someone would scream out.

"If you see it you won't forget it, that's for sure."

Of course the girls would be either scrambling to get off their chairs, or holding their dresses down or whatever. Larry would stand and say to the audience, "Don't worry folks. This little girl may look a little upset, but believe me she's not. Just last week she brought in her own quarters."

It would usually end when someone would yell out that he got it, and someone would say "You cock-eyed bastard, I think you got mine." Nothing was ever scripted or done like a regular comedy bit. It was just crazy fun. The bit would end as quickly as it had begun. We scramble off the floor and go back to serving the tables.

There was another bit we did to the ladies. Most women carry pocket books. When ladies would come in to sit at the bar, they'd usually lay their pocket books down. That took up precious counter space. What we did, was to tell them to hold their bags for a moment. Reaching under the bar, we'd produce a hammer and a large nail, and to everyone's surprise, we'd drive the nail into the bar's edge. Then we'd take her bag and hang it on the nail. We'd quickly follow that with," Do you want to check your coat?"

Most thought that we'd drive another nail for their coat, and would say yes. The bartender would then reach over and snatch her coat. Folding it in half he'd yell, "Number four thousand, two hundred and six", and toss it to the next bartender. Any one of us that was close enough to participate would join in. The "Number four thousand, two hundred and six", would be repeated over and over, until the coat, rolled up into a ball, disappeared into the kitchen. She'd then be told, "Remember your number, Lady, because we got a shit load of coats in there." If the girl protested, saying that her coat was expensive, we'd say something like, "Are you kidding me? That looked like a two dollar special from Herbage's imports down on Third Avenue. Not for nothing, Lady, but, if you paid more then three dollars for that piece of shit, then I think you'll enjoy our food. We cater to schmucks."

The bar top was uneven and scarred from nails and other abuses. Into the bar's surface, Louie had imbedded two Quarters. They appeared to be loose change. Unknown to all except those who worked there, the Quarters were wired to an electric outlet under the bar. The juice was controlled by a switch that was only accessible to the bartender. If he saw a drunk trying to pick up the Quarters that had been soldered and bolted, he'd throw the switch. The electric jolt always shocked and scared them. We'd tell the guy, "Leave the money alone. It belongs to the electrician, and he'll be right back."

We loved playing with drunks. If you had a guy sit at the bar, who was really over-the-top drunk, this was the perfect gimmick. We'd use our Whiskey Sour shaker glass. There are two pieces to the shaker. One part is clear glass while the other is stainless steel. We'd approach the drunk and say, "Let me buy you a drink. How would you like a nice Whiskey Sour?"

When he agreed, we'd set the two parts of the Shaker down on the bar, and then into the glass section we'd pour some whiskey over ice, adding sour mix as we did. Then covering the glass portion of the Shaker with the stainless steel top, we'd combine and raise them over our head, shaking vigorously as we asked, "Is that shaken enough?"

By this time the drunk would be licking his lips to get at his free drink. He'd watch intently as we poured the shaken drink into a glass. We'd place a cherry on top of the foamy concoction, and slide it to him. He'd raise the glass to down it and would look a little surprised when he received no booze for his efforts. The reason he never tasted any of the sour, was that we'd taken a bar towel and stuffed it into the stainless steel portion of the shaker. This would absorb all the liquid in the drink as we shook it. So he ended up with nothing but a foamy glass of ice. We'd then look him in the eye and say, "How was it?"

They'd usually say that it was great. We'd ask, "Would you like another?"

"Sure", one guy said, as he almost fell off the barstool, "I think I can handle it."

There was a large bass drum on the wall above the bar. There was a handle that hung over us that we could pull to beat the drum. There were other handles for bells and air horns and spiders that we could drop on a table. We even controlled jock straps that way. Sometimes you could do something simple that would really impress the people. Like if someone at the bar asked for a drink and requested extra ice, we'd hold the glass up and throw an ice cube at the base drum. The ice made a loud boom as it struck and bounced back at us. We'd catch it in the glass every time, acting like it was no big thing. If someone requested more ice, we'd just grab two-hand full from the ice bin, and throw it at his glass. If he wanted a coaster, in the same manner we'd grab a stack and instead of throwing them at the customer, we'd aim at the rafter's just above their head. The noise and sight of forty cardboard coaster's flying about would startle everyone.

That went for water also. Sometimes we'd have a garden hose hooked up under the bar, and when shown to the patron, saying, "Did you ask for more water?" they would usually run like hell. There was also a large rubber snake that was kept under the bar. When dipped into the sink and brought up at eye level, a few quick wiggles of the wrist would make the rubber snake appear real. I recall one girl who fled so fast that the only way she stopped was when she crashed into the Juke box. Scared but unhurt, we gave her a big hand and a bottle of Champagne to calm her down.

There was another bit that we did with many variations. The premise was to stop the patron from retrieving his change, so that he could leave a big tip. One method was a large vise-like wood clamp. We'd stack the money and make a big deal out of screwing the clamp down tightly. Looking at the people next to him, I'd say, "He'll never get that loose."

Or, more simply done, we'd just drive a large nail through the money. The funniest part of this bit was when he'd try to undo the clamp. That's when we'd bring it to everyone's attention. We'd do that by standing in front of him having a conversation. It went something like this.

"You guys gotta see this. He's actually trying to undue the clamp."

"You gotta be shitting me. I've had some cheap bastards sit here but I've never seen one actually undue the clamp."

Turning to the sitting audience, we'd say, "Can you people see this cheap bastard from where you are?"

Now all the time we're talking to the crowd, the guy is struggling with the clamp.

"This is not the way to act in a fancy restaurant. Jesus, I'm starting to feel sorry for the guy. Maybe we should help him out a little, and take up a collection."

If it turned out that the guy was a sport and just left the money, we'd stand there and say things like, "Oh, really sir, you shouldn't have. You're much too generous. Never, in all our years here, have we ever seen anyone as willing to leave a tip as you."

Usually, the sport would leave the Club smiling, and feeling good about the tip.

The most dangerous one that we did took timing and caution. When a patron would throw his money down, you would, with one of your hands, sweep away his hand, and with the other, plunge an ice pick through the bills. Only once was someone injured. It put a damper on the bit, and after that it was rarely done. All these things preceded the show. That's why, unlike most Club's, you never got a break. If someone showed up at eight-thirty and stayed until three o'clock in the morning, they were never charged additional minimums or service charges. They could watch three shows, all of them different, all in one night. We were definitely the best bang for your buck in Brooklyn. I think all the years of operation proves that the people knew best.

Chapter 10

A Show On Wheels

The night I saw my first show, it was performed by Louie, Eddie, and Moose. Back then they only used one standup microphone on a stage that we rolled out of the backyard. The portable stage was maybe eight foot by six in size; enough for a snare drum, one microphone and three men.

The stage was quite heavy and was mounted on roller skate wheels. It was propped up against the wall in the alley, and at show time, at least two of us would upright the stage and then quickly roll it down the isle. Being extremely careful, we would position the stage while warning everyone to watch their toes. It would crash down with a tremendous sound which always was followed by nervous laughter. To have more room Eddie would lay a large sombrero on the bar behind the stage filled with doodads that he might use, and the show was on.

To make up for the loss of waiters, Louie sent me into the audience with an enormous Abe Lincoln top hat on. Printed in large black lettering was the word, "Drinks."

Having never seen the show before, I was not familiar with the material. Once they began, I found myself laughing the loudest. Louie would hear me, and say over the microphone, "Stop laughing, you son of a bitch, and sell some drinks."

So in the beginning, my job was just to replace Stevie Shades at the bar. The first weekend I worked, Louie had me sing *"I left my heart in San Francisco."*

It went over well. I would go on to sing that song every weekend for the twelve years that I was there. The thought of it sometimes made me ill. I was prone to getting sore throats and to this day I can only manage a moderate amount of singing. Even talking above a crowd I find difficult. Louie and the men could scream all night long and it never affected them. It always amazed as well as bothered me. As the years passed I found out that I suffered from GERD, which is a reflux condition. Screaming was the worst thing I should be doing, and yet I did plenty of it. I have no regrets.

As my first month passed, I was given a few songs to learn and told that I was in the show. I replaced Moose. That was the beginning of *The Three Slobs* as we were sometimes called: Louie, Eddie and me. Every week after that Louie would give me new songs to learn. I had always been good with jokes, but found I had to step it up a bit in order to keep pace with the show. Louie would always say, "I want it to be a war up there."

I thought we made a great threesome. Louie had the voice and guitar, Eddie had the face and the moves, and I introduced harmony into the comedy songs. I also introduced a couple of foreign accents they hadn't tried. At the end of the third show, Louie and I would sing some straight songs.

Things were quickly changing. Stevie Shades and Ralph had quit, as well as Cappy. It was their time to move on. I worked the bar fulltime for six months and then found a day job. Needing someone to replace me during the week, I brought in Johnny Nibs.

Johnny Nibs, as we called him, was a neighborhood guy, whose family rented from my father. He needed a job and I knew Louie would like him. Johnny wasn't the type to get up on stage and make a fool of him self, but nonetheless had a great sense of humor. One busy night, I'm on my way to the kitchen when he grabs me and says, "You see that girl at the corner of the bar. She's a hooker and only wants five dollars for a blow job."

So as I'm passing her to get into the kitchen, I say, "Only five for a blowski, right?"

The girl almost choked on her drink. Upon seeing her reaction, I glance over at Nibsy and he's bent over laughing. With his big dimples indenting and his eyes squinting shut, I knew he had gotten me. So what do I do? I turn back to the girl and stupidly say, "Err. Only kidding."

I ran after Nibs, but by the time I got to him, I was laughing too. He came from a family like mine. They could have a party over a pot of coffee. I loved them all. Johnny Nibs replaced me and took over, not only the bar but also a little lunch trade that had sprung up. That moved me into a waiter's position. When Louie expanded the Club, he needed another waiter, and I passed that job on to my best friend, Larry.

Larry became my best friend and next door neighbor when we were seven years old. We were only four days apart in age, and from the first meeting we found we had a lot in common. Mainly, we liked to goof off and be funny. Even when we were in the same class in Grammar School, we were notoriously bad. One day we cut out of school at lunchtime only to rethink our move. Knowing we had made a mistake, we, instead of making it better, compounded our error.

At one o'clock, when we should have been in class, Larry decided to call up the principal. Instead of apologizing and making up a story as any ten-year-old would, he told her," Don't sell our seats, sweetheart, we're on our way home." That remark didn't go over too well with Mrs. Walsh.

There was a book kept in every class that was strictly for the teacher's hand written entries about the class. At the end of the school year, the teacher would read aloud all the commendations that the children had received. She would also read aloud the reprimands that some had gotten. Larry and I were on every page. If it wasn't talking or not having our homework or sneaking out of class, it was something funny, and I remember the feeling of thinking we were pretty good at screwing up. Nobody did it better. That was when we were ten years old. Since then we had really honed our skills.

Lou wanted to know what Larry could do and I told him that he spoke Italian and some Spanish. He played a little guitar and Harmonica and was very good on the bugle. He was a talented story teller and could sing. I added that he'd worked as a carpenter for most of his years. That could translate into handy man for Louie. I thought that would help him get the job.

Louie met with Larry and they hit it off. Larry said that Lou asked him to do something funny. He recalled to me that what he did was rather crude and not that funny, but Louie's keen eye for raw talent seen something that he liked. Larry began as a waiter but eventually became part of the show. But that's another story.

Chapter 11

Larry, Quick on his feet

To accurately describe Larry, you'd have to start with the obvious. He's a big guy. After digesting that, the next words out of your mouth would be he's a very funny guy. After talking with him for ten minutes you'd see that he was smart and good looking.

Being a smart comic requires that you've got to be prepared for anything. You must learn and store material so that whatever comes up, you'll be ready for it. A big part of comedy is to be able to spot and seize an opportunity for a laugh. It's absolutely essential for success. Larry was terrific at seizing the moment.

One Saturday night, the Club was jumping as usual. The juke box was playing, the waiters were working their tables, and the noise level was moderately high. The Cigarette smoke was thick enough to cut. Sal the doorman was keeping the line of people in check, allowing into the Club only a table at a time. Sal knew how to space out the entrants, and when the time was right, he'd announce them.

"Table of four", he would holler. When he did, the sitting customers would look to see what was going to happen. Well, instead of whistles and air horns blowing, one night the place became incredibly quiet. There, standing in the doorway, was a guy who dwarfed Sal, who stood about five foot five. The man stood six foot ten inches tall.

Larry, who was approaching the bar to get drinks, stopped in his tracks. Putting his tray down, he approached the man with his stomach sucked in and his jaw thrust forward. The audience laughed as they watched him try to transform his robust shape into one of a body builder.

He didn't stop moving until he bumped the man. Suddenly, they were chest to stomach. The big man looked down as Larry began to lay down the law.

"You better not start any trouble, Shorty. You better watch your step…or else."

The big man, who was a foot taller and much wider then Larry, answered, "Or else what?"

Larry instantly countered by answering, "Or else what? Or else…this."

He began to dance around the man throwing jabs and hooks, imitating a punch drunk prize fighter. Larry, now knowing that he has the Clubs attention, drops down to the floor and begins punching the guy in his knees, saying as he does, "First I'll give you one of these, and then I'll give you one of those," and on and on he goes until, finally, appearing exhausted, he collapses onto the floor. The people are laughing at the ridiculous scene before them and watch intently as Larry feints brushing him self off and wiping his brow.

"And if that don't work", Larry states, "Then I'll call my brother Junior."

Well, that was it. The big man was seated and the Club went into its normal flow again. About a half hour later, Larry is once again at the bar getting drinks, when the door opens and Sal announces, "Table of Four." Larry looks to the door and as unlikely as you'd expect, there standing in the doorway is another guy standing six foot ten inches tall. Without a second's delay, Larry screams, "Junior, you're here."

Quickly putting down his tray, Larry forcibly grabs the big guy's hand, and pulls him to the table of the first giant. Instinctively, the first guy stands as they approach. Larry puts himself chest to stomach once again. What happens next is amazing. The second big man sandwiches Larry between the towering duo, and then the two big men, who don't even know one another, spontaneously sense that what they're doing is funny, and press Larry between them like a grape. All the time this is happening, the crowd cheers the duo on. Larry, undaunted by their response, never stops ranting.

"That's it Junior, give him another one, that's it! First, give him an uppercut and then a jab."

Finally, the two giant's part and Larry drops to the floor. Once again, Larry drags himself to his feet, dusts him self off, and says as he wipes his brow, "I guess I showed them who's boss. I think I could use a drink." The two big men laugh and shake hands as the crowd cheers. We never had trouble with the really big guys. Their personalities matched their height. There must be a calming sense of freedom knowing no one in their right mind would want to fight them. These two had a good time being a part of another Country Club moment.

Another thing that Larry did beautifully was the Spanish accent. Because he spoke Puerto Rican style Spanish, it seemed more authentic when he'd throw in phrases that only the Puerto Ricans in the audience understood. It endeared Larry to the Spanish people, and made his stories more believable.

Larry was responsible for a show that stands out in Louie's mind as one of our best. Early in the show, Larry did a Spanish joke that went over really well. As I followed with a joke, Louie whispered to Larry to do another Spanish joke. Larry, always a comic, decides on the spot to do a Jewish joke, but surprises us by continuing with the Spanish accent. That went over so well, that it led him to do Irish, Italian and every subject and nationality that we covered, using a Spanish accent. The show lasted an hour and a half and he never changed accents. However, he did change hats.

Much that we did was accentuated by physical props. We had rows of hats hidden in the rafters that encircled the stage, and changing hats throughout the night was common practice. If we were doing Jewish Jokes, Louie would say, "Quick, Look Jewish, look Jewish." We'd simply reach up and in a flash we'd be wearing black fedoras with long dark hanging curls. In only a moment, we'd change hats and take on a new identity. You name it, we'd look it. Try to imagine a six foot tall, two hundred and seventy pound man, standing in pajamas with a Hasidic style hat on, then, speaking in a thick Spanish accent, doing a Jewish joke. Imagine a Swedish joke, or maybe a black joke. It was extremely bizarre and very effective. Props and accents really worked for us. That night Larry utilized everything we had, and really shone.

Chapter 12

Cement Mixer

In 1945, two musicians of that era, Slim Gaillard and Bam Brown, wrote and recorded a song that was a hit nationally. The song was called "Cement Mixer," (put-ti put-ti). We did a parody of it, and it went from just a parody to a great visual bit, due to my being a nosey garbage collector.

When I worked for Clarke Forklift Company, I routed all of their mechanic's trucks so they could do repairs on forklifts that were rented out by us. One day I was throwing something into the trash, and spotted some old oil pressure gauges that had been discarded. I took a moment and went in and retrieved about a dozen of them. When I arrived at the Club Friday night, I went to work on an old wood milk box that Louie had, and attached the dials to it. The box began to transform into looking like a machine. Next, we took a pair of inflatable legs, complete with panty hose, and gave them a nice spread-eagle stance, straight up and out of the box. Then, in between the legs, different items were placed out of sight of the audience. There was a wig, a ladle, salt and pepper shakers, different pieces of fruit including cherries and a real banana that Larry would peel and eat during the bit. The original story line of the record had a background sound that imitated a cement mixer. The original song went, *"Cement mixer, put-ti, put-ti."*

Our rendition sang, "Cement Mixer, pus-sy, pus-sy." As Louie and I sang, Larry would bring out the box and place it onto a bar stool that we had on stage. Standing behind the box, with his head between the legs, Larry would then go through all the different items in the box. His facial expressions and body language was sensational as he poked and pulled and stirred and tasted the brew between the legs. It wasn't only lyrically funny, but visual and musical.

I cannot recall one man who worked at the Club, who wasn't brought in by another worker. Louie hired by word of mouth. Eddie, although a simple guy, was an adventurer. He owned a sail boat and also had a pilot's license for small air craft. Being associated with airplanes is where he met Pete.

Pete the Bartender, as everyone knew him, was a World War Two Navy Veteran, who, we had heard, was credited with shooting down a number of Japanese air planes during World War Two. Some of us felt that he had actually talked them out of the sky, with his "Did you hear the one about," routine. The man could tell joke after joke and never tire of it.

Pete was of average height and very handsome. He looked impressive behind the bar, especially since the wooden drain boards on the bar's floor added a few inches to his height. One night he was asked to jump up on stage and do a few jokes while we attended to some emergency. Anyone who's performed on stage will tell you that it's a lot more difficult to do then to watch.

Well, Pete jumped up on stage okay, but caught a case of the jitters and lost his nerve. We all laughed, because, here was a guy who could talk the ears off a dead monkey, and yet the sight of an audience made him a stuttering idiot. We rescued him by starting the show and wouldn't you know it, when he got back behind the safety of the bar, he went back to his old ways. He was another gem of a guy who worked at the Club for years.

Another Gem was Crazy Tony. Tony, Larry, Johnny Nibs and I grew up together. Called Crazy Tony, he was always a lot of fun to be around. With many tattoos covering his arms, he was short and stocky with prominent features. His hair line had receded into a narrow widow's peak. His large brown eyes looked about to burst, as if he was always expecting something to happen. He had a clown-like smile and chubby cheeks that perfectly surrounded his bubble nose. Everyone loved his nose, because he could actually play it.

By pinching one nostril, he could strum the other while emitting a high pitched shrill. The sound he produced was like that of a steel guitar. His rendition of Hawaiian music was fabulous. Another thing he did well was to sound like Lou Costello. He'd crack us up by doing the "Hey Abbott" routine in Italian. He was a good dancer and he had a terrific voice. Here was a ball of talent that, I'm sorry to say, had never performed on our stage. Unlike most of us, he didn't stay at the Club very long, moving on to do other things.

Another guy that moved on was my brother Andy. I'd mentioned him earlier as the man, who by mistake, had washed Louie's huge coffee pot. Andy worked in the kitchen and I guess he was with us for almost a year. At the end of the last show, we'd usually do a few straight songs for the crowd. Louie would introduce us as *"The Mother's Brother's."* We'd sing, *"If I Didn't Care,"* which, was an old hit done years earlier by *the Ink Spots.* Louie even had him do a few bits with us. There was one in particular that he took over from Moose. It went like this.

This bit took some preparation and time. It would start with us being on stage and Andy interrupting us. He'd appear right in front of the stage and begin by saying, just a little louder then necessary, "Who ordered the food…who ordered the food?"

Louie would stop playing, and say to us, "Is this the new kitchen guy?"

I'd say "Yeah," and Lou would continue, "What's wrong with this guy. Why's he so loud. He doesn't have to stop the show just to deliver a hero sandwich. Is this guy your brother?"

I'd say "Yeah. He's probably a little nervous…it's his first night working here. I'll talk to him later."

Andy would then take a full loaf of Italian bread, and holding it suggestively with two hands near his belt, he'd sing, "I got a hero here. It's a real big hero."

Louie would once again yell for Andy to shut up and stop interrupting with the show. As Andy disappeared into the kitchen some of the waiters would be cursing and throwing coasters at him. That would seem to be the end of it.

We'd continue the show uninterrupted for about fifteen minutes, when all of a sudden Andy would be in front of center stage. He'd be wearing a cigarette girl's tray around his neck and he'd yell, "Rubber balloons here…get your rubber balloons." He'd continue repeating this line until Louie's guitar playing ceased. We'd stop the show. Again, now with the room in complete silence, he'd repeat, "Rubber balloons here, hey, get your rubber balloons."

Louie would once again go into a tirade, while also apologizing to the audience. Larry and I would do the same, and under this barrage of insults from us, Andy would look up at Louie and say, "What's wrong?"

Louie would say, "What's wrong? There must be something wrong with your brains. Don't you see all the noise you're making?"

Andy would say, "How do you see noise? Then sheepishly, he'd say, "But Boss, you told me to hustle the room."

Louie would counter with, "Sure, I told you to hustle the room… but not during the show."

All eyes would be on Andy as he slowly glanced around the room. Then, looking like he just woke up, he'd say, "Oh…You mean…The show is on?"

Once again he'd retreat to the kitchen. The audience would get a kick out of all the commotion, as the waiters and bartenders joined in, some throwing ice cubes and toilet paper at him as he retreated.

Time would pass and we'd invite a young girl onstage, usually one who was getting married. There were many jokes, questions, and comments from us, about weddings and honeymoons. The girl would be on stage about ten minutes when Lou would stop what he was doing, and say, "What was I thinking? You know, we do this every week and we're used to the pressure, with almost three hundred people staring at us with the lights glaring and all. This poor girl isn't used to this. Why, she could get nervous and pass out."

"Pass out," we'd say. "That would be terrible."

I'd look at Larry and say, "I don't know about you, but I wouldn't know what to do if she passed out." Larry would say the same. Louie would then turn to the girl and say, very tenderly, "Don't worry sweetheart, I just completed a course at NYU that teaches you exactly what to do in such an emergency. You see, the reason that some girls pass out is because their blood stops flowing freely through their veins. So, what we have to do is to get it flowing again. Jeez, Sharon, you look about as tall as I am, so I may need some help doing this. Do you guys want to give me a hand with Sharon?"

"Lou. You tell us what to do, and we'll do it."

"Okay then, now pay attention fellas, and do exactly what I do."

Turning to the young girl, he says, "Not you sweetheart, you don't have to do nothing. Just lay there like a latke. And don't worry sweetheart, because if you pass out, I'm sure that when we get done with you, you're gonna come too. All right fellas, here's what we'll do to get her blood flowing again. First, we'll rub her arms," and we'd repeat, "We'll rub her arms."

"Then, we'll rub her legs," Again, we'd quickly repeat, "We'll rub her legs," followed by Louie saying, "And then we'll"….. that's when Andy would appear yelling loudly, *"Rubber balloons, get your rubber balloons."*

Larry would suddenly have a rubber balloon clamped in his mouth, stretching it towards the girls face. Everything came together quickly. It was a bit that required pin-point timing. The audience never expected a condom sale. It always worked well.

Another guy that deserves a mention is Stevie Shades. The word was that he left the Club because he wanted to retire. I think he was twenty six at the time. Although I'd replaced him behind the bar, he still would return for a drink and a laugh. He was always popping in to see us, and usually he has a girl on his arm. On more then one occasion he'd informed us that he was engaged. We never believed him.

Another thing about him was that he always looked the same. When he worked behind the bar he'd wear a pair of pajamas, with sleeves rolled up and sunglasses on. He always wore the sunglasses.

When he came to visit us, he'd have on a black suit, black tie and white shirt. He could have passed for a classy undertaker. He was a thin man of medium height who never showed anger at anyone. No matter what was going on, he'd always be laughing.

On one occasion I saw him without his sunglasses and I gotta say that that was one scary moment. He had the smallest eyes I'd ever seen. I once remarked that he had the best eye plan of the group. All he had to do was remove his glasses and we'd all chip in to buy him another pair. Now that's a good plan. He was always a great guy and always helped out if we needed it.

Tommy once made a good remark about Stevie. Cappy was visiting the Club one night, and he spotted Stevie sitting in his usual corner spot. Cappy told Tommy to get Stevie a drink. Tommy commented, "Oh, this is fucking rich. We got one guy who isn't paying buying another guy who isn't paying. They'll both leave a tip so the only one not making any money is Louie."

So during the years that the Club flourished, guys like Pete, Tony, Stevie Shades and Andy contributed in many ways.

Their attitude and readiness to laugh at anything enhanced what the Club was all about. Simply put, it was their charisma that carried over to the people. After having their own experience at the Club, customers would return with the thought of putting their friends through the mill. When they did, they became in essence, a part of our crew. They were on our side, and their mission and ours became the same. To make them laugh. It was a no lose situation.

It was very rare that we'd encounter someone getting mad over a bit. When that happened, the audience would actually turn on them, not liking the idea that they couldn't take a joke.

"Throw the bastard out," someone would say. "If you can't tell what kind of a place this is just by looking at it, then you got to be an idiot. Don't let this guy ruin the whole night. Throw the bastard out."

What a great place to perform. The show wasn't only the three guys on stage, it was the bartenders, the waiters, the ceiling and the walls. It was the signs and the props and the over-the-shoulder remarks that flew by at top speed. Especially, it was our loyal customers, who were always a big part of the show. I can close my eyes and picture two young guys that used to frequent the Club a lot. Their absence was unexplained until I received a letter from them. They had signed up for the buddy system and joined the Army. They wrote me that they were both serving in Viet Nam.

In their letter, they included a song one of their Army buddies had written. It was a parody of "The Green Beret," which had become a monster hit. The parody wasn't very good, but I wrote them and thanked them for trying to help out. Here were two kids, thousand of miles away, and they were still a part of the Club. It inspired Louie to write a parody about the Italian Army. He called it, "The Yellow Beret."

During the Viet Nam War, we had a lot of servicemen visit the Club. On a few occasions, we even went to The Veterans Hospital before going to the Club, and put on a show there. Guys who were withdrawn in the hospital would seem to come alive at the Club. I've seen guys with no hands crushing ice cubes with their steel prosthetics, just to be funny. I've seen men with only one leg, dancing in the aisle. I think the Club served as a great release for them. I often thought about those two guys in Viet Nam when we sang "The Yellow Beret," and, I cannot recall ever hearing from them again. I wonder about them, and pray that they made it through that terrible time.

Chapter 13

Tommy, a/k/a, Uncle Festus, Mister clean

One of the most memorable of our crew was Tommy. When I began bartending, Tommy was my partner and my mentor. He was well built and of medium height, with a full head of dark hair. He had large expressive eyes that complimented a great smile, and an easy laugh that had just a tinge of indelicacy to it. I'd often hear him address a girl with a "Yes dear," only to turn away to say something crude, like "Your mothers ass," or "Get the fuck out of here." When he said those remarks, his voice would trail off, making it almost impossible to hear. Then he'd laugh loud and generously, eliminating the literal meaning of his words. Any threat of an insult was removed. What was left was a laugh. He was basically a good looking tough guy, and the ladies loved it.

Tommy proved to be the best at controlling bachelor parties. When the bachelors began to get out of line, he'd resort to an old school method that reminded me of the immigrant fathers who ruled the roost with a look. He would cock an eyebrow at them and stare. That look said everything. We rarely had trouble at the Club.

I respected Tommy for working hard. He went to college full time while working in his uncle's butcher shop and tending bar on weekends. School and two jobs paid off, and eventually he built his own graphic arts business, designing menus for many of the large restaurants and cruise ships. He never married and at some point in time, I guess his success dictated that he quit the Club, and he did.

A few years passed, and then once again Tommy showed up at the Club. There was something different about him. He was wearing a hat. He looked out of sorts and in a bad mood. He was drinking heavily. It only took a few moments for us to notice that Tommy had a problem. Large clumps of hair were missing from his head. He had a condition known as Alopecia Areata. We never knew the cause of it, but word was that something of a personal nature had traumatized him. The hair loss was not only permanent, but also total. Eventually, not even an eyelash was left.

Unlike today, the sight of a completely bald man was uncommon. In the nineteen sixties, long hair was in. The Beatles had created a new look. If anything, a bald head looked comical.

Tommy had a thriving business in Manhattan. He attended meetings that required him to be looked upon as a serious man. Ignoring all the side glances and snickers wasn't easy and took a great effort on his part. He was a strong and confident guy. Perhaps the combination of living alone and trying to handle his new found problem pushed him towards the Club again. It was inevitable that he return to us. It had nothing to do with finances, it was all about coping. Tommy was not going to crumble or lose his sense of humor. I've heard it said that what goes on in the head comes out on the tongue. Tommy was no exception, and would speak his piece.

He was working in Manhattan one day and as was his manner, he was dressed impeccably in an expensive suit and hand painted tie. He was riding in an elevator on his way to a business meeting, when the door opened and a very prominent figure got in. It was the movie mogul, Otto Preminger. It must have been quite a surprise to have two completely bald men meet in an elevator during the hair craze that was sweeping America, but here they were. Each man eyed the other and nodded, smiling pleasantly. Finally, Otto Preminger spoke.

"It looks like you're copying my style," he said, indicating Tommy's baldness with a nod.

Like I said before, Tommy had a gruff side to him and you never knew when it would surface. He had a way of puffing up his chest when confronting someone, and he did just that as he spoke out.

"Let me ask you something, Mister Preminger. Do you have hair on your balls?"

The movie giant was taken back for a moment, but managed to answer, "Well, of course I do."

Tommy looked Preminger in the eye, and replied, "Well, then, I guess I'm not copying your style."

That was Tommy, funny and to the point. Otto Preminger had met his Waterloo.

Tommy's appearance changed as time went by. He gained some weight and gave birth to a double chin. On occasion he drank a little too much Scotch, and one night in particular is memorable.

He arrived at the Club ready to work but clearly was in no shape to do so. Louie told him to go home and sleep it off. Tommy took a drink and then staggered out of the Club. Instead of getting in his car and leaving, he walked the thirty feet or so and entered the Club's kitchen entrance. Moments earlier, Louie had left the bar to go to the kitchen. As Lou entered the room, there was Tommy with drink in hand, swaying where he stood. Tommy looked at Louie and said, "Jesus Christ, you again? Do you own this fucking bar too?"

At the Club many referred to him as Mister Clean or Uncle Festus. He worked at the Club far longer then I did, and was an attraction in his own right.

The funniest moment that involved Tommy, happened during one of our shows. Louie, Eddie and I were on stage. We were doing a song and near the end of the song Eddie produced a toilet plunger. He was standing on the edge of the stage and dead-panning the end of the routine, milking the laughs. When the song ended, Louie told Eddie to stop acting like a fool and to get rid of the plunger. As Eddie glanced around the stage to find a place to put it, Tommy stopped at the front table to serve drinks. Without any thought or rehearsal, Eddie reached out and in one swift motion, slammed the plunger onto Tommy's head.

It was a million to one shot that a plunger could stick so well, but it did. Maybe it was the combination of Tommy's sweating baldness that allowed the plunger to lodge itself so perfectly, but it stuck like glue. I have never seen an audience regardless of who was performing, as fractured as our audience was that night. Everything seemed to stop. The three of us on stage lost it completely, and crumbled to the floor with the air knocked from our lungs. What made it that much funnier was that Tommy never once reached for or grabbed at the plunger. Instead, he just looked up at us and then slowly turned to the audience. Whichever way he turned, the plunger followed. He then very quietly resumed serving the drinks. He never even smiled as he asked the table he was serving, "Who gets the scotch and soda?"

As the roar began to quiet, Eddie composed himself and, reaching down, pulled on the plunger. It resisted at first and then finally gave way with a loud pop. The red ring that encircled Tommy's head was met with roars from everyone. Tommy looked at the crowd and said, "Your mother's ass," laughed, and went back to the bar. That was another great moment I'll never forget. If people were asked who they remembered at the Club, it's a good shot that they'd say "Mister Clean."

In 1967 I was working for Clark Forklift and one of the mechanics approached me and said that he'd seen the show, and was interested in getting a job there.

I asked him what he could do and he answered, "I play the guitar, the Harmonica, and the drums. And I can sing."

I introduced him to Louie, and he started out in the kitchen. Eventually he became a waiter and did get into doing the shows. We always laughed because it turned out he didn't play the guitar, drums or Harmonica very well. Nobody cared, because none of us played anything well. He had an easy demeanor and was very likeable. At least he could play the drum using the sticks. I was strictly a brush man. I was not a drummer but could manage to keep a decent beat. As bad as I was, I faked it for twelve years. The only real musician we had was Louie. Everything was built around his guitar. The mechanic, who was short and slight of build, became known as Little Tony. That wasn't very evident to our customers, until we matched him up with Big Dick.

I met Big Dick one night when I was tending bar during the week. I was always conscience of men who showed up at the bar alone, thinking that they might be a bad drunk. When the door opened, I immediately saw that the entire entrance was filled in by a human form. He appeared to be wearing shoulder pads and I could see that he was very tall. The next thing that stood out was his nose. I could see that it had been broken a few times. It appeared this was not going to be a good night.

He ordered a beer and we started to talk. He told me he was just discharged from the Marines and I knew how they liked to fight, so things were going downhill. It turned out that I was wrong on all my assumptions. There's a saying that you should never judge a book by its cover. It's true. Dick turned out to be a great guy who came to work in the kitchen, serving Louie's famous meatballs. A great sight to see was Little Tony standing with Big Dick. Dick would usually wear short shorts, combat boots, a pajamas top and sunglasses. Tony loved white pajamas with red hearts all over them. What a pair they made.

Dick stayed a while but then also moved on. It seemed that most of us who stayed for a long period of time had some interest in being known as a part of the Club. It was the only Club I knew where the waiters wouldn't take a tip to move you to a better table. The first come, first served rule really applied there. I doubt that even Louie would believe that we'd go that far, but I swear, many the time I'd tell someone to put his money away. If they wanted a good seat, I'd tell them to come early. If they still wanted to tip me at the end of the night, I more then welcomed it. Back then it wasn't mandatory that you had to leave a tip. If you sucked as a waiter or a comic, you got nothing. If you, on the other hand were good, you'd get something. Clearly, this was a part of the work ethic of the times, and in my view, the way it ought to be.

Chapter 14

Tony and Stewie

When Tony Burdo began working at the Club, he was quite young. I always had the feeling that he'd follow in his father's footsteps, and I think that was born in me when I saw him sitting in his garage at about thirteen years of age, practicing his guitar. He looked determined to learn it, and as it turned out, he became a terrific guitar player.

As I think back, I cannot recall if he just showed up one day as the boss' son and did little things to help out, or if he came to the Club with a specific job in mind. I remember him doing most of the jobs like bussing tables and bringing food out from the kitchen. Bussing tables at the Country Club was a little different then the methods used in the finer night spots. At the Club, you would simply remove the glasses and card board plates that were used for food, and then with a mighty sweep of the hand, you would dump everything else to the floor. Many times, in order to speed things up, I would take the table and just flip it on its side, bring it upright, wipe it with a damp rag, place a minimum card and tuna fish can ashtray down, and I was ready for another group.

Tony did everything that was expected of him. He even kept the flow of talent coming to the Club. He had a band and they played gigs wherever they could find the work. A few friends from the band would show up to hang out, and watch us do our thing. I remember one pleasant looking kid who was borderline chubby, with dark curly hair and an easy manner. He would serve food and help out with some of the bits wherever and whenever he could. He was always smiling. I think he smoked a little too much pot, which is probably why he was always smiling.

Pot smoking was something the younger generation did. We were different. I was from the street gang era and they were the hippies. If you smoked, you were either a hippie, or going to College where you had explained to you all the benefits of smoking pot over drinking a glass of Scotch.

Personally, when someone would offer me a joint, with their face aglow and contorted with the pain and effort of holding the smoke in, I would say to myself, do I really want to look like that or would I rather look like Cary Grant, with a babe on my arm and a Scotch on the rocks. To me it was no contest. That's what I get for having no education.

That thought brings me back to my first day of boot camp and my first smoke break. Our drill instructor lined us up and asked who among us was college educated. Only a handful answered. Then he asked about high school. About half the men answered. Then, he called for the dropouts. The rest of us answered.

"All right," he ordered, "Give me three ranks of men here. I want the college boys in the front, with the high school boys behind them, followed by the dropouts. Now here's what you do. I want the college boys to walk down the street picking up all the cigarette butts they see. I want the high school boys to follow them and pick up all the matches they can find. What about the dropouts? Well, I want you stupid bastards to follow them all, and watch, and try to learn something."

Believe it or not, in my neighborhood, during my era, if you smoked pot you were considered a junkie. Junkies in my neighborhood caught beatings, so none of my friends smoked pot, that is, not until they improved their education. They say you should watch and learn. Isn't that the truth.

Well, Tony watched and learned. He mirrored his father's talent and looks. The only difference in them physically was their height. Tony was taller. When I left the Club in 1977 to join the Fire Department,

Tony brought in a guy from his band to take my place. His name was Stewie. When I asked Tony what instrument Stewie played, he said, "He doesn't play anything. He just dances and falls off the stage."

Well, that turned out to be the truth and I must say, no one did it better. He would have made Jerry Lewis proud. In all the time I knew him and worked with him, I only heard him do one joke. I couldn't recount it, if I wanted to because it was in Yiddish. I'm not sure if the audience knew what he was saying, but they always laughed. What I liked about him personally was that he approached the men in the show with respect, appreciating what we did. The comments and playing with the audience was a natural gift that everyone had, but when it came to the show, you had to be prepared. He knew what it took to do the show.

To start with, I think Stewie appeared tall because he was so skinny. He sometimes would show up clean shaven but usually he'd have a beard growing in, looking a bit scruffy. When he did, he looked like the real Yiddish Mc Coy. He had two sticks for eyebrows and a large grin. He was a master at making faces and contorting his body. If there was any weakness in his verbal abilities to tell a joke, his physical attributes completely over shadowed them. He made everyone laugh.

He could do things that were just plain silly, like put a shirt on and end up with his two arms lodged within the same sleeve. He could spin like a top. But more then anything else, he could fall off the stage. When Stewie was doing a show, he would work his way towards the edge of the stage. This was done in a calculated step by step approach, and not just one giant step and he's there. He got there by dancing and twirling as the night wore on and before you knew it, he was close to slipping off and getting killed. If you watched the audience, you could see their apprehension growing. You could see the worry on their brow. I also think that they rationalized, who would take a chance and fall off the stage, just for a laugh. No one in their right mind would do that. So, what we ended up with was a confused audience. You could see the tension mounting as the show continued, with Stewie seemingly not paying any mind to his precarious situation. He appeared to be the only one who was not concerned.

When the scene became commonplace and the audience a little more relaxed, that's when he would make his move. With one sweep of his arms flailing he'd miss a step and crash to the floor, and then drop down off the stage, rolling and sometimes bringing the snare drum and cymbal with him. It was always noisy. There were screams of horror as the worst was expected and then he'd crawl back on stage, only to fall again. Genuine relief was felt by all and you could always hear someone say, "I knew he'd fall off the stage."

Tony and Stewie developed many bits together which they'd do on the floor. One of the bits was for them too come out in basketball uniforms, throwing a basketball around to the music of The Harlem Globetrotters. As they worked the crowd, passing the ball to and around them, Stewie and Tony would inevitably end up under someone's table, or on their backs squirming around the floor. They were as loose as a dish of Jell-O.

Another classic bit they developed was used as people entered the Club. Stewie, on crutches and with his leg in a cast, would greet the people as they entered. There would be the usual bells and sirens and then there was Stewie, looking quite sick and uncomfortable. When the noise settled he'd say to the people in a soft voice, "I'm so sorry. I really can't move faster due to my accident. I've lost a lot of strength."

Tony and Stewie would slowly lead them to a table and while balancing himself on the crutches, Stewie would pull a chair out for one of the girls to sit. As he turned towards the man he'd fake losing his balance, and while falling, he'd reach out for him. The mark would usually grab Stewie to help stabilize him, and that's when Stewie would really go to work. First, he'd lose his crutches. Then, with the man struggling to hold him up, Stewie's feet would begin slipping and sliding on the floor. Tony would be yelling for the customer to grab Stewie. Stewie would then secure a good grip on the beltline of the man's pants, and using all his strength and weight, he'd fall and pull. As Stewie went down, so did the marks pants. Usually the mark would realize what was happening and try to stop it, but with Stewie yelling for the man to help him, the mark, now desperate, would have only one hand free to hold Stewie up, and the other to stop his pants from hitting the floor. It was a great bit, with the mark's friends laughing the most. It never failed.

The hours I worked as a New York City Firefighter, were such that I couldn't stay and be a part of the Club. But, on occasion, I'd get a call from Louie, asking if I could stand in for him for a weekend or two. On those occasions, when I'd do the show with Tony and Stewie, I would pray that Stewie didn't kill himself with those unbelievable falls.

Tony and Stewie worked really well together. Tony's singing and Guitar playing filled in the void made by Louie absence. You could always count on them to give it their all. They were quite a pair.

Chapter 15

I, Me, Myself

It was never my intention to make this book auto-biographical. Rather, I wished it to be a biography of The Crazy Country Club and all who worked there. Being that I worked there, let me tell you a little about myself.

I grew up blessed with a wonderful family. I cannot emphasize that enough. I was born and raised in Brooklyn, in a neighborhood called Windsor Terrace. No one I've ever met from Brooklyn has ever heard of it. If you looked at a map of Brooklyn, we'd be situated between Prospect Park and Greenwood Cemetery.

Born in 1940, I was raised by The Greatest Generation, a generation that didn't coddle their kids. They were a generation who themselves had it so tough growing up, that they thought we were lucky to live in this country. We said The Pledge Of Allegiance in school and respected our elders. So the core of my growth period was solid. But nothing is perfect. Education in my home, and for that matter, even my neighborhood, was not impressed upon us or demanded by our fathers. Our parents wanted us to do better and get a good education, but if it turned out we didn't, well, that was our choice. You had to live with the consequences.

For the most part, I felt I had a pretty good aptitude for school, but it just didn't fit in with my plans. School was much too serious a place for me. I was a clown who wanted to laugh. After all, my dad had little education and he seemed happy. We always had a home and a car. We always had food on the table and compared to the stories of his up bringing, well, we had it pretty good. I knew of no one who had more fun than he. He loved to sing and play the guitar, and would enjoy that with his family every chance that he could. There was always time for a song.

Now previously I had talked about my Mom and her terrific sense of humor. Her ability to tell stories was wonderful. I truly hope that you've retained what I wrote about her in a previous chapter, because I don't like to beat a dead horse. Being redundant is not the way to popularity. Outside of joke telling and loving a good laugh, I find no evidence of any talent what so ever, on my mother's side of the family. They were generous and fun loving but not one of them could sing a note. So I looked to my father's side.

I don't really have a family tree on my father's side. It's more like a branch here and a branch there. But here's what I think and know. My dad's father was a singer and a comedian. He was in an act with my uncle, and they were known as Carroll and Florio. He started out in Vaudeville with people that made it big, including his best friend, Irving Berlin. Some of the guests that my grandfather had at his first daughters Christening were, Fannie Brice, Jimmy Durante, Eddie Cantor, and many others of that era. I never met my grandfather so I cannot say if he was a great talent or not, but according to my dad he was an absolute riot. He played some piano and loved the drums. He could sing in any key and could throw his voice across a room. He was excellent at harmonizing and had a million jokes. He was a short, dumpy, fearless man, with blonde hair and blue eyes. His nick name was Happy John.

My dad's mother was born in Chicago. Her family was loaded with characters. Her brother Pete De Grace was a prize fighter who later went into the restaurant business. When I was thirteen, I met him at his restaurant on Long Island. It was called Delmonico's. Another brother, Joe De Grace, was an entertainer who traveled the circuit during the early part of the century. He toured Europe seventeen times. He also was part of a two man team known as Joe Webb and Jack Burns. My aunt told me that they often sang on radio. Jack Burns went on to be a big star in silent films.

My grandmother had an operatic voice. All accounts say that she was a terrific singer. She was singing at a wedding that my grandfather was attending, when he suddenly got the urge to join her on stage. She was totally shocked when he suddenly began to harmonize with her. They say opposites attract. She sang Arias and he sang parodies. After a short period of dating, they married.

Genetically, any interest or talent that I have goes back to my father's side. My father studied violin as a child, which brought him to the ever popular guitar and Mandolin. He worked private parties and had his own four piece band when he was sixteen. They played at some of the smaller Catskill resorts and anything else they could find. He also took small jobs with my uncle Bill. My father told me that the worst gig they ever played was in Staten Island. It was a wake for an old Irishman. Dad said that when they got there, they spotted an old guy sitting in the corner. Every once in a while someone would put a lighted cigarette in between his fingers, then drink his drink and replace it with another. It turned out that the old guy was the stiff. He was a hated man. They were throwing him a farewell party, and cursed him the entire night. Dad said the night was eerie, but that they made good tips.

My father's cousin Arthur Gallo, who was raised in the same house with my dad, had only one occupation. He played professional saxophone all his life. He had one son, Paul, who followed on the classical Clarinet. Paul graduated Julliard and went on to play with a symphony orchestra. Music was a big part of my father's life. In his house, they had a piano, a set of drums, a violin, a saxophone, a trombone, and a guitar. So, musically, my roots were there.

One cousin of mine named Frankie Basil was a singer and I understand he did very well, as an opening act. Also, another cousin, Jed Mills, became an actor which included television and Movie's. He killed *Joe Pesci* in the movie *Casino*. He swung a mean bat.

Now it's my turn. As a child I was shy when it came to performing. I did attend Arthur Murray's singing school for a few months. The instructor there was overly friendly to me, and I thought he had intentions of abuse on his mind. Afraid to tell my father, I quit the school. My singing went into a low profile and was reserved for mostly family and friends.

At fourteen, I fell in love and wrote my first song. I recall three of my friends and I, huddled in the bathroom of the local American Legion Hall, practicing. We finally mustered up the nerve to sing it Doo Wop style, but after that, I went back into hiding. I lacked the confidence, and truly felt I wasn't that good. Secretly though, I sang a lot and wished to be more involved in it.

Years passed and I joined The Air Force. It was there that I met an airman who ran the service club. His name was Bob, "Blacky" Blackstone. He had an extensive history of entertaining which went back to the early age of three. I also met a fellow named Orville Kenneth Barnes The 3rd. We called him O K Barnes. He was a great guy and a talented guitarist. I met him at the motor pool, where, during a driving course, he had managed to bring his guitar. I began to harmonize with him as he played and sang. He was very musical, but knew little about harmony. We joined forces and created an act. We called ourselves The Star Lighters.

We became deeply involved with doing shows at the service club. We also traveled with a troupe to hospitals, prisons and clubs of all kind. Our troupe was a very diverse group. We had comics, magicians and singers. We gained experience and were doing okay. Barnes and I entered the Air Forces "Tops N' Blue" contest. We won in California, but lost at the next level in Delaware. We then started to get gigs that paid fifteen dollars each, a hefty sum in those days, and were beginning to make nice headway in that circuit, when suddenly, he was transferred to Iceland. So the extent of my showbiz career is not one to brag about. I wrote some songs, sang with some groups, and did some comedy. Not much else happened until I went to the Country Club. So the question of the day is this. What do I think of me? Here's my honest answer.

When it comes to singing, I don't possess a great range. I do think I have good tone and diction. People enjoy my singing. I have a terrific ear for music. On some rare occasions at the Club, Lou might start an unfamiliar song that just wasn't in the right key for me. Instead of stopping the song, he'd just tell me to listen and then change keys. I was able to change keys with him, and not lose a beat.

I'm still too shy when it comes to dancing. I'm not a show off. I feel much more at ease when it comes to doing comedy. In order to sing well, you have to possess a God-given talent. It's not the same thing with being a comic. There are funny people and there are people who can be funny. When it comes to telling jokes, I'm very good. I don't see myself as a funny person, but, I can make you laugh. It depends on things like the chemistry that I'm feeling as I interact with people. Some bring my funny side out. I think that's what happened at the Club. I learned a lot there through trial and error, and now I can structure a joke like a story, including everything that's needed and excluding all the extras that are not. My timing is excellent. Being on stage with a microphone in my hand seems to empower me.

I won't interrupt or try to out-shout anyone. If I'm out socially and find someone that's overbearing in their ways, I'll just let them do what they want and eliminate myself from the conversation altogether. I become easily bored with no–talent-loud-mouths.

However, if you're willing to share the floor and also listen just for the sake of having a good time, then I'm your guy. There's nothing I like better then being with funny people. To me, there's a difference between someone who's funny, and someone who's trying to prove that he's funny. If you're funny, you'll see it in the people's eyes. You shouldn't have to prove anything. I always felt that the Club and I were meant for each other. The conversations and the turns they took from normal to blue humor were ones that would and could happen in my home, sitting around the kitchen table. Such was the humor that I enjoyed. I recall once, that at a wedding reception, a man was about to tell my father a dirty joke, and suddenly stopped, nodding his head in my direction. My father smiled, and put his arm around me, and told the man to tell his joke, indicating that at sixteen, I was old enough to enjoy with him the things that he knew I already knew. To him, it was just a joke, and was meant to be enjoyed.

So armed with everything I've mentioned, I was a shoe-in at the Club. Twelve years of hard work, twelve years of fun and games, meld together into twelve years of an unforgettable experience.

The Club was where I met my wife. In 1966, a young girl graduated High School, and with three of her girlfriends, all of them armed with phony proof of age, came to the Club for a night of celebration. Being a girl who loved to dance Latin, they came to the Club that night to see Joe Cuba and his band.

That pretty girl was Kathy Simineri. We hit it off big time from the first moment we'd met. Eighteen months later we were married and that's when she related this story to me.

She had heard from a friend that at the Crazy Country Club, if you asked the bartender if you could look into the box, he would bring a wooden box over with a door on the top. What they had heard, was that there was a cutout in the bottom of the box, and that the bartender would actually have his penis exposed inside it. They never asked for the box, however, they'd sat there hoping someone else would. Of course none of this was true, but such was the way the stories went.

So, in summing up my experience with the Club, I would say this. It afforded me a way to increase my income, which benefited my wife and son. It allowed me to be myself and to feel the self worth that you get from performing on stage. It afforded me a place where I could shine. It made me unique in a small way, and I really appreciate that. I made many friendships that still continue on today, so, you ask, would I do it all over again? You bet your ass I would, and if you don't mind, I'd like to hold the bet.

Chapter 16

A mixed bag of tricks

The most difficult part of writing about the Club, is trying to explain how and why anyone would come to celebrate his own special occasion, knowing, that complete strangers might be joining in. It's not like being at a restaurant and everyone sings along to "Happy Birthday To You". It's quite different. The material is novel, the setting is bizarre, and the staff, are zany. Putting yourself in that position, is really throwing caution to the wind.

This goes to show the great amount of confidence the public gained through the word of mouth advertising that was done by the public themselves. Although you knew you'd have to be careful, you also knew that you wouldn't be hurt.

Every night, it seemed, we had at least one bachelor party, but usually the groups would number at least five. Not to be outdone, the ladies would also come to celebrate their upcoming marriage's. There were other events like birthdays, anniversaries and engagements. Occasionally, we'd even get a divorce party. There were military Service Men on leave, some of them with horrific injuries suffered in Viet Nam. I can even recall one bridal party, white wedding gown and all, coming in for a few laughs before the honeymoon. That was a sight to be seen.

Some people just came for the show. How can I possibly describe the show using only the written word? I don't know if I can. You've got to help me by using all of your senses. I mean, the Club smelled like an Italian deli, sounded like an insane asylum, and looked like a yard sale at a barn. Every wooden chair and table was painted without any design except that it was multi-colored. Although it's hard to picture, it actually blended together quite beautifully. It was easy to take.

The show was fast and full of snide remarks, often employing double entendre. The music that we played had a driving basic rhythm of guitar, bass and snare drum. Many an introduction had a walk of single notes to lead us into a song. Regardless of the age of our customers, the sound they heard always seemed familiar and easy on the ears.

The show had many parodies, some of old nursery rhymes, some on current events. We shied away from little. The jokes we did were directed at different groups; the Gays or the Clergy, the Jews or the Christians, it mattered not. If it was funny, we'd do it. Much of our material was built around the everyday problems that we all face, be it our children, our Doctor's, plumbers or landlords. We'd invite people from the audience to join us on stage. Sometimes, we'd have people come up to sing a song. Some were very good. Once we had a comic ask if he could do a few minutes, and Louie, against his better judgment, allowed it. The man took the stage and pretty much cursed his way through his routine. It was immediately clear to us, that he didn't have a clue as to what we were all about. If the Club would have been built on just raw language, it would've never gotten off the ground. Although we joked about everything, we never encouraged abhorrent behavior. I cannot recall any jokes about taking drugs.

A typical night at the Club was never typical. We had a female dummy sitting in the corner of the bar, next to the phone booth. She had on a tight sweater with two light bulbs for tits. There were other dummies too. Some times in the early part of, or at the end of the night, we'd sit a few of them in a corner. When someone would sit near them, but were unaware that they weren't real people, the bartender would make his move. He may say something like this.

"I told you girls that you owed ten dollars for the drinks. Pay up now or I'm gonna through you out on your ass."

When the dummies didn't answer because they couldn't answer, the bar tender would whip out a pipe, and say, "I friggen warned you," and with that he'd whack them on the head.

It was all about reactions. It was as funny as the people made it. Many times some of the patrons knew what was going on and just sat there salivating for the moment when it would all come together. They were in on everything. Many times they'd set their friends up.

People brought in things to help us out. There was a terrific sign hanging above the bar that someone brought us. It was about four foot long and ran on electric. Originally it was to be a Spanish Matador strumming his guitar advertising Spanish Sangria. Well, Louie took the sign and plugged it in, then turned it on, and we waited. The Matador began to strum his guitar. Louie looked at it, and said, "No good." Reaching up he grabbed the electrified arm and bent it down as to now make the Matador scratch his balls. "Now that's more like it," he said, as he chuckled and walked away.

Another time a plumber brought in a toilet bowl, in tact and in working order. Louie took the bowl and set it against the wall near the front door. It stood there for weeks without anyone saying a word about it. Louie then came across a few sheets of plywood and on the spur of the moment he nailed three sides up around the bowl. Then he came across a door and so he then attached the door to it and wrote Ladies Room on it.

One day, a drunken woman entered the Club, and almost walked into the phony bathroom. If she had peed or done worse, it would have been a misery to clean, not to mention a health code violation. Louie feared she may do that in the future so he devised a plan.

He took a garden hose and ran it from the cellar up through the bar, around some walls and finally lodged the hose out of site. The nozzle ended up in the base of the toilet. They waited.

About a week later in walked the women, drunker then ever, and before they could stop her, she entered the fake toilet.

"Quick," Louie yelled to the bartender, "Turn it on, turn it on."

With the twist of the wrist the water began to flow. The water spray was sometimes hitting the ceiling it was so strong. After more then a minute, with water cascading out the door, they turned it off. They watched as the door opened and the women came out. She was dripping wet; her cloths soaking, her hair completely flattened. As she closed the door behind her, she turned to Louie and said, "Shit…You better tell the owner he's got a hell of a leak in there."

With that she left and never returned. Once again, some of the patrons were in on it.

Another time someone brought in a regular fire hydrant. It was painted red and of course extremely heavy. Not sure where it would fit in, he put it outside. At that time Louie was still doing some construction on the new building, and outside on Seventh Avenue there were some rather large holes in the sidewalk. Innocently, he stuck the hydrant in one of the holes and thought nothing about it.

In the early sixties the Fire Department was very busy in Brooklyn, and it just so happened that the predominately factory neighborhood was a good place for vandals to torch automobiles.

One late afternoon Louie hears sirens and stepping out his door he sees a car in flames. Now let me say that firefighters don't view car fires as anything very serious, however they do burn hot and smoky, usually drawing a crowd. As a firefighter the one thing you don't want to appear is inept. After all, people will watch you and say to themselves, I hope these guys know what they're doing.

Well, that day, at that fire, there was an alternate chauffeur not familiar with the neighborhood. Dropping their hose line near the fire he moved the engine to within ten feet of the hydrant. He hooked up his high pressure hose and waited for the Captain to call for water. The only problem was that he hadn't checked the hydrant.

With the crowd watching, the Captain called for water. They waited as the chauffeur opened the operating nut to get water and of course nothing happened. The hose never inflated. The Captain called again. The crowd watched and began to snicker. The Captain got very pissed very quickly and called for booster water which is an emergency supply that they carry on the truck. The Chauffeur realized his screw up and with the five hundred gallons on board they extinguished the fire. Louie was questioned but said he had no idea where the broken hydrant had come from.

"Matter of fact", he told the Captain, "I'd like you to get it off my property."

Louie said the water department was notified and eventually came and installed a new hydrant. Believe it or not, they never removed the old one, and people wondered why he had two hydrants in front of his bar. Who would believe it.

Sometimes you could play havoc on the customers with very little to work with. For instance, Louie had an outside patio in the old club which was never used in the winter months. There was a door which led to the patio so what Louie did was to make up some signs, which read, Ladies Room…follow the arrows.

When customers came in and were seated, they'd remove their coats and warm up with a drink. When women had to go to the Ladies room the waiter would say, "Out that door and follow the signs."

Now outside in the frigid cold the ladies room signs had been placed as to form a large circle which in fact would bring you back to where you started. Of course the women wouldn't be wearing their coats, so they froze their asses off to say the least. The funny thing was that when they were asked how they found the ladies room, not one of them would admit that they never found it.

Eddie had another toy he liked to play with. It was heavy, brass metal cannon about two feet long that he would tie down on the stage. The cannon would be filled with black powder and there was a trip cord attached to fire it with. If the juke box stopped playing and things turned quiet, Eddie would pass by the stage and fire the cannon. The report from it was not only thunderous but the flame that followed was both long and bright. It was a relatively safe bit to do, noisy but safe. And then this happened.

One night as we were setting up the Club before we had customers, Louie asked Larry to change a light bulb above the stage. Larry stood on a chair and after unscrewing the old bulb, he reached down and put it in the barrel of the cannon. It was just a matter of convenience. After replacing the bulb he was called into the kitchen and completely forgot about the old bulb.

As the night wore on a lull in the noise begged for the cannon to be fired and Eddie was always ready for that. Unaware that a projectile of glass was lodged into the barrel, he nonchalantly passed by the stage and pulled the cord.

The sound of the cannon seemed louder than ever as the bulb flew across the room at supersonic speed and smashed into the wall. Fine glass particles showered down on anyone near it. Remarkably, no one was hurt and no one knew what happened. We were very lucky that night, and never let Larry change another light bulb.

One customer told me that every time the Clubs door opens, it's like I'm at Coney Island and I'm waiting my turn to get on the Cyclone. You've heard stories and been told about outrageous things that have happened, and although they're hard to believe, here you are waiting your turn. You look around you, and all the people seem normal. You wonder if you look normal to them.

We had a group of people from The Bronx that owned a bagel shop, and they always brought us bagels shaped as Dildo's. We never asked them to, they just did it. If you didn't want to be stared at, you had to eat these bagels when you were alone. Offering one to a lady customer created quite a bit of giggles.

The fun at the club started when you got on line. It continued when the waiters screamed out for you to follow them because the show was about to start. Before you know it, you're given a seat, an insult, and a drink. Looking around you can see that everyone's laughing. The waiter is holding a Bagel Dildo in front of your girls face and saying, "Remember Honey, I give you a big tip now, and your boyfriend gives me a big tip later. Right?"

He then rips a piece of the Dildo off and handing it to the girl, says, "Taste it sweetheart, if you like it I'll give you a whole one."

With that he turns and runs away, yelling, "Showtime everybody, it's Showtime."

Ed and Crazy Lou take a coffee break

Ed, Sal, Nibsy, Shades, Otto and Tony

Larry, John, Nibsy, Big Dick and Otto

Ed, Larry, Nibs, Dick and Otto

Larry blowing taps

Eddie pulls a falsie out of a girl's blouse on stage

Author Big John behind the bar

Lou And John on stage

Tommy blowing up an unsuspecting skirt

Stewie being himself

Tony, Lou and Stu. What a body

Lou, John, Larry, Nibs, Eddie and Sal Da Doorman

Lou, Larry and John on stage

Stu working the crowd

Postcard of the old Club

On stage, 1970. Left to right, Ed, Lou, John, and Larry.

Eddie, Lou, and John. The three Slobs.

Eddie, Larry, and John setting up a table for one.

Eddie, John, Larry…Late show.

Lou, Tony B., Stu and 'Lil Tony

Crazy Country Club, 1963

Lou watching Cappy having a high ball.

Ed, Lou and John.

Ed, Lou, and John

Tony, Stu and Lou doing Cement Mixer

Lou and John, tipping their hats to a lady

Lou and John, giving them what they want

L to R. Eddie, Sal, Nibs, Lou, Stevie Shades, Big John and Lil' tony

L to R. Ed, John, and Lou. What is that thing?

Santa Larry, Lou, Nibs and Sal. A quiet moment before the doors open. 1970

L to R standing. Ed, Nibs, Lou, Stevie Shades, big John.
Sitting. Sal Da Doorman and Little Tony.

Standing. Sal, John, Stevie Shades. Sitting is Big Dick and Otto.

Big John working the Floor.

Big John. Behind the bar. 1965

Lou, Ed and John

Stu, Choking the chicken

Tony, Lou and Stu on stage

Lou, Tony and Stu, another show

Scott, Tony, Nibs and Stu

Pete, Lou and Tommy

Carl and Pete

Nibs, behind the bar. O.K. Barnes singing a tune. Barry on the Bass

Crazy Tony. He could play that nose.

Larry with Barry and a customer

Lou, cigar in hand, before the show

Chapter 17

Show Time

Louie checks the time. We're slightly behind. He signals to me and Larry, and we give our last round of drinks out and immediately go into the kitchen. Lying on the counter is an assortment of jip sheets and notes about the audience. Louie tells us to take a piss and to give our bar tabs to the other waiters. We briefly go over the list of people who are to be mentioned in the show, and what songs we'll do. Most of that preparation is already and automatically registered in our heads, as certain favorites stand out.

The order of the show is to have no order at all. We will simply discuss an opening and a closing number, and that's it. Louie has always demanded that the show be a war of one liners, jokes and songs. The idea is to overlap material at such a rate, that the audience would find it hard to keep up with it. Involving the audience is paramount to the operation, and so we personalize everything. Our strategy affords us great leeway in addressing the audience.

Also, the club utilizes little in the way of fanfare. No one introduces the act. When the time is right, Louie will yell out, "Show time." That's the signal. The waiters will echo his words, the plug on the juke box gets pulled, and "The Three Slobs," as we are sometimes called, will make our way onto the stage. A single switch is thrown and lights over the stage illuminate it, and that's it. The show is on.

On Fridays we did two shows, and on Saturday, we did three. We never repeated the same material on any given night. There were times when Lou tried to expand his business into the week. For a while, he had a three piece girl's band playing on Wednesdays. Then he tried bringing in popular Latin groups like Joe Cuba. The Spanish were great dancers but lousy paying customers. We always found empty whiskey bottles in the men's room. They brought heir own so the profit margin was cut drastically. It appeared that the Club had one main function, and that was to make people laugh. During a hot Latin song, Joe Cuba would stop his band and say, "Now let's hear the Crazy Country Club guys."

We'd blow every horn and ring every bell. The funny thing was that it sounded pretty good. Joe Cuba was a good sport.

The late show always ended with some straight songs and then the place would empty out. We'd lock the door, throw on all the house lights, grab a drink and split up the tips. We usually made between sixty and eighty dollars a night, and that's including our ten dollar salary. Then we'd stack the chairs and move all the tables against the walls. Sweeping up the mountains of debris and toilet paper, which sometimes reached three feet in height, took a while. Then we'd mop the floors. The transition from entertainer to janitor was sobering.

It's very difficult to give you a blow-by-blow account of what took place night after night, but after doing the show for twelve year's, I can honestly say that what follows is a good representation of a typical night. The shows were done by many combinations of men; Louie, Eddie, Larry, Little Tony, Moose, Otto, Stevie shades, Tony, Stewie, and me. All of us had something different to contribute to the act, and I think all of us were funny. Reaction from our audience confirmed that.

When the show was announced, some in the audience clapped. Others adjusted their chairs to get a better angle of the stage. The stage was large enough for the three of us, the drum and bass, and a guest. We also had a bar stool and a triple dresser on stage that held all of the doodads.

The level of clamor usually dropped, but the sound of talking and bar glasses tinkling, as well as a large scoop of ice being deposited into a tub, was obvious. Dead silence just wouldn't fit into the atmosphere of the club.

Louie would sling his guitar over his shoulder and begin the motions of fine tuning it. I would move my standup snare drum into position, and set up my microphone. I had already placed a large Scotch and water on the triple dresser behind me. Louie had a black coffee. Larry had a gin and tonic.

Larry would drag his large standup Bass from the kitchen and noisily set it onto the stage. He's capable of making music with the Bass, and unlike Eddie, fills in the basic rhythm that the act needs.

All of us secure our sheets of paper regarding the audience members that are going to be mentioned. There's a good mixture of occasions to be addressed. There's a Bachelor Party of eight cops and a girls bridal group from Flatbush. There are a few birthdays including an eighty year old regular. There are lots of guys in uniform and some are with nurses. There's one girl who claims she's a Playboy Bunny. Add to that the array of nationalities represented and there's plenty for a show. Now the war begins.

As Lou steps up to the microphone, I begin to tap on the drum like I know how to play it, with an occasional switch to the cymbal. I use the brushes to play, and upon reaching what I think is perfect tuning, I smile at Larry. Of course everyone knows you can't tune a broken down snare drum. Louie looks to the audience and quietly says, "This is what I get for calling the union. You ask for musicians, and you get morticians. It's impossible to get good help anymore. Maybe if I ignore them, they'll go away."

I peek around Louie and say to Larry, "I got nowhere to go. Do you?"

Larry answers that if he leaves by himself, he's afraid he'll get lost, which is what his father's been telling him to do for years. He looks pathetic when he speaks, and his eyebrows have an unusually high peak in the center of his forehead. His large brown eyes and wrinkled brow help convey the innocence of a child. The audience quietly laughs.

I look at Louie and say that I think we're staying. Louie looks helpless as he tells the crowd that it looks like he's stuck with us. So far, all is relatively calm and not rushed. The audience gets comfortable.

Lou leans towards the microphone and quietly says, "Before we start, I've got to ask one question?"

Larry asks, "What's the question, Lou?"

Louie says, "Are their any Italians in the room?"

The room erupts with clapping and cheering. The Italians roar their approval of proper recognition. As it subsides, Louie begins the war. He says, "I thought so. I could smell the fucking garlic from here."

The audience reacts by laughing at the Italians, which is what we want, because the three of us on stage are Italian American, and we don't want anyone feeling like they're the only ones being picked on. If we could do it to ourselves, we could do it to anyone.

"Now that we cleared that up, I have to ask another question. Are there any Jews in the house?"

Louie asks the second question with just a little more gusto. Again the room erupts with applause.

I lean into the microphone and say, "I once heard someone say, that when Jews go to heaven, they go feet first. Is that true?"

"I never heard that," says Louie. "Why would you say that?"

"Don't get me wrong," I say, "I love the Jews, and as a matter of fact, my uncle was going out with a Jewish girl. One night I got home a little early and I heard a little noise in the living room, so I made my way quietly in to take a peek. What I saw was like a religious experience."

"You turned Jewish?"

"Not, exactly."

"Your nose grew?"

"Thank you, but it's big enough."

"Well, what happened?"

"There, right in front of me, was this beautiful Jewish girl spread eagled on the couch. She had both her legs straight up in the air, and she was screaming, 'HOLY MOSES I'M COMING.'"

"Unbelievable," shouts Louie. "You mean she was actually going to heaven feet first?"

"That's right. And I'll tell ya something Lou. If my Uncle Charlie wasn't holding her down, I think she would have made it."

Lou looks at the crowd as if to say, my apologies.

"As you can see, it's gonna be a long night. Now that we know that we've got Jews and Italians here, I want to say something before I forget. I want to thank all the guys in uniform for making us proud. A lot of countries have armies, but ours is the best. I felt that I just had to say that. Now, to continue, do we have any Greeks in the house?"

There is a little clapping from the crowd, but nothing in comparison to the Jews and Italians.

"You see what I mean", says Louie. "That's not much of a hand for Greece, and do you know why? That's because Greece doesn't have an army."

"You gotta be shitting me," says Larry.

"Yeah", I say. "I thought every country had an army. Why don't the Greeks have one?"

"The reason that the Greeks don't have an army, is, that the Greeks can't get anyone to go to the front."

"Now that makes sense," says Larry.

"That's because you see everything ass backwards."

"My problem is", says Larry, "Is that I'm actually part Jewish."

"Really, which part?"

"My mothers part…the part that can't cook."

"If the Jews learned how to cook," I announce to the crowd, "half the restaurants in New York would close."

"Well, if you want to, you can make fun of their cooking, but you can't make fun of their army."

"What do you mean", says Louie. "Do you think their Army is rough and tough?"

"That's right. The Jews have the roughest, toughest army in the world. Did you see what the Jews did to the Arabs? Maroone…six days and the war was over. That's what I call tough."

"Wait a minute," says Louie, sounding a little like Jimmy Durante. "That war in 1967 was an unfair war. That's why the war ended in six days, not because the Jews were tough, but because it was unfair."

"What was unfair about it?"

"It ended in six days for a few reasons. Number one, the Jews acted as if all their tanks were rented from Hertz and had a return date. Number two, everyone knows that a camel can't run as fast as a Cadillac, and number three, the Jews didn't want to pay the fucking overtime."

Larry says "Now that makes a lot of sense."

Louie looks at Larry and says, "Everything makes sense to you, even nonsense. All right, so now that we know we have Italians, Jews, Greeks, and the Army here, who else could be visiting tonight, you ask? Well, how about a Playboy Bunny? That's right. We have a gorgeous blonde that you'll meet later."

"And," I say, "Not to be outdone by a Bunny from Manhattan, we have six pussies from Flatbush."

"What a deal," screams Louie. "Six girls for the price of one. And, listen folks, if you're like Larry, and have trouble with arithmetic, just count the tits, and then divide them by two."

"It's much easier that way," says Larry shyly.

"And I have to say," says Louie, "That these girls are perfect in every way."

Larry nonchalantly plucks a few strings on the Bass, and says, "Well, these girls may be perfect in every way, but those Bunnies…sometimes they do strange things with their cloths."

Louie step's back, and say's, "Do you mean their fluffy tails and cute rabbit ears? That's not strange, that's their costume."

"I'm not talking about their costume. I went out with a Bunny once, and had an awful experience. When I got into bed with her, I found out that she had her panty's on backwards."

"I've never heard of anyone doing that. Her panty's on backwards? I hope you didn't stand for that?"

"Of course I didn't. What kind of a man do you think I am?"

"Jeez, Larry, what did ya do?"

"What did I do? Boy, oh boy…did I chew her ass out."

I wait a moment, look at Larry and sounding a bit serious, I say, "I had a cousin with a similar problem."

Louie says, "Ya mean, Larry chewed your cousin's ass out too?"

"Nah, I mean when he was becoming a citizen."

"John. You have cousins that are citizens? Not in this country, I hope."

"Here's what happened. My uncle Primo, who's an expert on becoming a citizen, explained the three questions that are required to get your papers. First they ask, "What's the name of the greatest country in the world? Of course, the answer is, America. Next, how many states are there in America? The answer is fifty. And the last thing they want to know, is, the colors of the flag. We all know they're red, white and blue. So anyway, my cousin Vito, who only went to the third grade, told my uncle he had trouble remembering things, so my uncle showed him a trick. He told him to write down all the answers on the inside of his shorts. This way, when they asked the questions all he had to do was look down and read the answers."

"Your uncle sounds like a genius. What happened?"

"Well, my cousin did what my uncle had told him, and everything seemed fine. The only thing he did wrong was that he put his underwear on backwards."

Louie, still sounding like Durante, says, "He made the fatal Bunny mistake."

"That's right, so when they asked him 'Which is the greatest country in the world,' he answered 'Fruit of the Loom.' When they asked how many states there are in America, he answered, 'Thirty four to thirty six.' And when they asked him for the colors of the flag, he said, 'Yellow dots with brown stripes.'"

"That only goes to prove that you can't get into this country flying by the seat of your pants. What surprises me is that your cousin could read at all. He is Italian, isn't he?"

"Well, sure, he comes from Italy, so the odds are fifty-fifty, that he's Italian."

"Wow," Louie says, "You must take after your uncle Primo. You said fifty-fifty like you know all your numbers. What do you know about sixty-nine?"

"Sixty-nine? Oh, that's when you and your wife don't see eye to eye."

Larry jumps in with, "Did you hear about the Frenchman who was doing sixty-nine when the phone rang? He looked down and said to his wife, "Pick it up honey, it's on your end."

Louie says, "Pick it up Honey, it is your end."

"I knew a Frenchman", Larry says, "Who was very content and well rested. Why, he'd fall asleep as soon as his feet hit the pillow. The stupid bastard didn't know what a period was, and boy, oh boy, was his face red."

"Speaking of periods...let me take a moment to introduce you to Sharon Levine. According to my notes and her sister Lynn, who's her maid of honor, Sharon's going to get married next week. Hey Sharon, we want to ask you some questions."

"Oh, shit," says Sharon. Her bridal party screams out to get her on stage. Louie looks down and says, "What do you say, sweetheart...you want to join us on stage?"

"Yeah," Larry yells out, "There's nothing to worry about. Remember Sharon, you can't get hurt by anything soft...so you'll be safe up here."

"Let's go everybody, let's get Sharon up here."

Sharon was clearly game. She slid her chair out to the roar of the crowd, and made her way to the stage. Her bridal party stood and cheered her on. As she made her way to the stage, we sang to the tune of *Here comes the Bride,* our own words of *Here* the Bride comes.

Chapter 18

Sharing the spotlight

Sharon is helped onto the stage by Larry and a stool is provided for her to sit on. Louie reads from his paper the names of all the girls and the fact that Sharon is Jewish and from Flatbush.

A funny thing would happen when someone was brought up to the stage to join us. It seemed to give that persons crowd not only the permission to speak up, but also the nerve to readily become a part of the show. A heckler would be out to hurt you by interruption, but this was different. They really helped us out by bringing out things that we might have missed, and that could open up a whole new set of subjects. That was exactly what we wanted. Also, their good time was made even more memorable by their participation. In short, they'd have a night to remember.

We get the girl comfortable and welcome her to the show. Louie explains that we'll just ask a few questions and that there's really nothing to this. He begs her to relax.

"Is your boyfriend Jewish?" Louie asks.

"Yeah", says Lynn, the maid of honor. His name is Hal and he's a doctor."

"Oh", Louie says, "You're Sharon's sister, Lynn. What do you do for a living, Lynn? Are you also a doctor?"

"No, I'm a secretary." The conversation with Lynn can easily be heard throughout the club. Louie tells the audience that Lynn is not only Sharon's big sister but also her Maid Of Honor.

"A secretary? Well, Lynn, I don't know how to say this, but I think you better change your job before it's too late. You should look into changing your occupation."

The focus is removed from Sharon and all eyes are now on Lynn.

"I don't want a new one," she says. "I like working in an office."

"Oh, and I'm sure you're good at what you do, but I'll tell you something, Lynn, the way things are going, you'll be out of work in six months."

Lynn laughs. "That couldn't happen. I work for a large firm and they never lay off anyone."

"Did she just say that she never gets laid by anything large and firm?"

"No Larry. She said she works for a large firm, and that she won't get laid off."

Larry says, "She must know what she's doing. She looks like a smart girl."

"And I'm sure that she is, however, I just read something in the Times that maybe she missed. Here's the problem. You see Lynn, IBM just came out with a new computer… that sucks, so by January you'll probably be out of work."

"That's right," I say…computers don't take lunch breaks, vacations or talk to the bosses wife. I think Louie's right Lynn. Get out now while you can still suck up to the boss."

Lynn screams, "Not me, don't do it to me, do it to my sister."

"Oh, listen to this," Louie says. "Now the Maid of Honor has turned into a pimp. Where were you when Larry needed you, any day last month?"

"Any day last year," Larry says. "I don't get enough sex. Hey Lynn, did you ever see one of those ice cubes with a hole in it? Well, I married one."

"His problem," I say, "Is that he married an Eskimo, and every time they make love, they rub noses. Four times last year he came down with sniff-less."

Louie says, "We all know that the cold can shrink things, right? In Larry's case, it was his brain. Wait a minute, I'm getting off-track. I want to get off Larry and back onto Sharon. Now, listen to me, bubbala. Jewish people often have problems that are unique to them alone. For instance, this wouldn't happen to an Eskimo, but, I knew a Jewish girl, who by the way was built just like you, who had a terrible problem. I tell you this in the hopes that you can learn something."

Louie looks serious as he adjusts his guitar so that he can use his hands in a more effective way when explaining his story to Sharon.

"One day, this Jewish girl that I knew, approached her grand mother and said, 'I don't know what to do with my Irving. We've been married for a month, and every night for a whole month, we've been making love.'"

"That's not a problem," the grandmother said, "what's really bothering you?"

"Well," the girl said, "my breasts are very small and Irving's trying to be extra nice, so he pays special attention to them. But all I can say, is, that after a month of nibbling and sucking, and squeezing and pinching, I'm so sore that I'm ready to scream."

"You shouldn't scream," her grandmother told her, "I've got the perfect solution. I had the same problem fifty years ago in Poland, and it worked great on grandpa. So here's what you do. Before you go to bed tonight, take a can of sardines, throw away the fish but rub the oil all over your breasts, and believe me, this old Polish remedy will keep him away. If it worked on grandpa, it will work on Irving."

So that night, the young bride did as her grandmother said. As Irving entered the bedroom and put out the lights, he ran and dove into the bed, landing as usual, with his nose buried between her breasts. After one big sniff, he suddenly stood up, jumped off the bed and hollered, "Wait a minute, Honey, wait a minute. Tell me something, are you too high, or am I too low?"

"I know another true story," I say, "that might help you out. I knew a young Jewish couple, who were one night making love in the living room. After about five minutes, the guy stopped moving, and looking down at his wife he said, Honey, not for nothing, but you're very, very, dry down there tonight. She looked up at him and said, Schmuck, move up a few inches, you're still on the rug."

"That's a true story," says Larry.

I crash down on the cymbal as Louie hits a few cords on the guitar and says, "Enough fooling around. Let's find out where they're going on their honeymoon." Louie looks at the small piece of paper he's holding and says, "It says here you're going to Puerto Rico. Is that true? Puerto Rico, what a beautiful place for a honeymoon."

Larry begins singing a song in Spanish, and then turning to Sharon, he says that he loves Puerto Rico. "Do you know why I love Puerto Rico, Sharon? Well I'll tell you why. I love it because it's so cheap to get to."

I say, "What are ya talking about, cheap to get to?"

Larry continues, "It's very cheap. All you need is fifteen cents…you get on the A-train, get off at one hundred and twenty fifth street, and bingo, you're in Puerto Rico."

"Wait a minute", Louie yells out. "Don't tell me that you're going to the Del Fuego Conquistador con Puto Del Rey. What an unbelievable Hotel. They got the greatest greeter on the whole Island. They got a midget who, as the people arrive, kisses everybody in the joint."

Larry hollers, "What a way to start the day."

I interject, "Yeah, they got a thing for midgets in that hotel. I remember once, I went into the men's room just off the lobby, and as I walked up to the urinal to take a leak, a midget stepped up to use the one right next to me. There was a guy on the other side of the midget, and suddenly, this guy began to shake violently. As he shook, he muttered, wa wa wa wa wa wa wa wa.

Almost immediately, the midget began to shake and call out, wa wa wa wa wa wa wa wa, over and over. The man looked down in amazement and said to the midget, "I thought I was the only one in the world who did that. Tell me, were you hit by lightning too?"

The midget looked up and said, "Not exactly. The reason I'm s-s-s-s-shaking is that you're p-p-p-pissing in my ear."

I pause by turning away and grabbing my Scotch.

"That hotel must be loaded with midgets," says Larry. "I was in Puerto Rico at that very hotel, and I saw a cop arrest a guy for screwing a midget prostitute."

"She must have been a little fuck," says Louie.

Larry continues without missing a beat, "Yeah, the cop was mad and told the guy, "I warned you three times not to come down here to screw any of the girls, didn't I?"

The guy climbed off the midget and said, "Ah, come on officer, give me a break, will ya. Can't you see that I'm trying to cut down."

"I'm trying to do you a favor," said the Cop. "What if you ran into your wife and she saw what I'm looking at, you with cream on the front of your fly. What would you do?"

"Oh, don't worry about that. She's not too smart. That happened once before, and I just told her that I ran into a midget eating a Canoli. She yelled at me for ruining a good Canoli."

"That's all well and good", says Louie, "but that isn't teaching this young girl anything. Like, for instance, the one thing that's highly recommended to newlyweds in Puerto Rico, is that they go on a Wind Jammer cruise."

Lou pauses. "This way, Sharon, Hal can just lay back and get blown all over the Island."

"I'd rather get blown on a dog sled," says Larry.

"Now you know why he married an Eskimo. He likes her moguls, and she loves yelling, 'You feel like Mush, you doggie, mush. Let me continue with some very valuable information, so I can help Sharon. For instance, Sharon, did you know that ninety nine percent of all doctors recommend that newlyweds take vitamins before going on their honeymoon. That's true, and the vitamin that they most recommend is made from chicken blood. Yeah, you see, they say it makes the men cocky and the women lay."

"We can learn a lot from birds. Like, Sharon, do you know why farmers put a cock on their roof?"

Sharon is laughing and says she doesn't know. I leans a little closer and yell, "Cause if they put a pussy up there, the wind would blow right through it."

"I love birds," Louie says, "and I love bird experts."

"You mean, like a cockologist?"

"Some people have a gift for these things. I was in a butcher shop, waiting my turn, when this woman asks the butcher for a Long Island Duck. The butcher hands her a duck and she takes the duck, spreads its legs and takes a big sniff. She then tells the butcher that this duck isn't a Long Island duck, it's from Rhode Island.

The butcher gets another duck and hands it to her. Again she spreads the ducks legs and takes a big sniff. This ducks from Texas, she yells out. Give me another one. The butcher does and again she says that this duck is from Ohio. The woman is now furious and tells the butcher that he doesn't seem to know his ducks very well. You must be new here because I've never seen you before. Where are you from anyway?"

The butcher turns around, bends over and spreads the cheeks of his ass, and says, "I don't know, lady. Why don't you tell me?"

Larry says, "You know for years I thought that Cock Robbin was a felony. Hey, I know a true story about two duck hunters. One of them stuttered a lot and the other one was spastic. One day they're out in a row boat hunting ducks, and as a flock fly's over the stutterer says, "G_G_G_GaGaGa, give me the gun." Bang!! He shoots, but he misses. A few minutes later another flock fly's over, and again, the stutterer says, G-G-GA-GAGI-Gi-Give me the gun." Again he misses. The spastic hunter says that's it. When the next flock comes by, I'm gonna try to shoot one. Suddenly a flock fly's over. The spastic stands in the rowboat and try's to take aim. His body is flying about the boat in frantic gyrations, his movements almost capsize the boat, but finally, he shoots. BAMM. He drops a bird which falls directly into the boat. The stutterer looks dumbfounded when the spastic screams, "I Got him right between the eyes."

"S_S_S_Sure ya did. And it's no wonder you got him. I mean... ya aimed all over the fucking sky."

"We can teach Sharon a lot of things, like, I use to think that Moby Dick was a Venereal Disease."

"I bet Hal the Doctor knows about Venereal Disease."

"Not to mention midgets."

"And some doctors have pets, says Louie. Did you ever hear of the Spiral Ass Bird? You haven't? Well, what an exotic bird that is. What's so unusual about the Spiral Ass Bird, is that it fly's in a circle so fast, that its Bill ends up in his ass. Louie pauses, then says, 'Which is exactly what I want my doctor to do with his bill.'"

119

Sharon has gotten to the point where she doesn't know who to look at. All three of us are firing lines at her so fast, that she's continually laughing. The reaction of her Bridal Party makes it that much funnier.

"Sharon, did you ever hear of the 'Oh, No, bird? Ya didn't? Well, let me tell you about it. It's got big, big balls, and short, short, short legs, and when it lands it hollers, Oh no, Oh Noooo."

"I went to my doctor to get advice for my honeymoon," says Lou, "and the doctor said the best thing I could do was to give my wife nine inches and hurt her."

"So what did you do?"

"I did what he said. I fucked her three times and punched her in the mouth."

Lou pauses. "Punching her in the mouth was the best part."

Larry takes a puff on his cigarette and with his chest out, and a smug look on his face, he says, "Last night, I made love to my wife, nine times."

Me and Louie both feint shock, and together we overlap statements, saying things like, "You got to be kidding...nine times, did you hear that Sharon? That must be a world record...I never heard of anyone doing it nine times."

Larry looks at the both of us and says, "It's true." Placing his hands behind his neck and pumping with his pelvis, he continues," Because I counted them. ONE, TWO, THREE, FOUR, FIVE, SIX, SEVEN, EIGHT, NINE....Boy oh boy he says as he wipes his brow, "That last one was murder."

"Last week, just to keep up with you guys, I gave my wife ten inches."

"I don't understand," yells Louie. "I gave my wife nine inches, Larry did it to his wife nine times, and now you say you gave your wife ten inches. How did you do that?"

"It wasn't easy Lou. I had to fold it in half."

"Hey Lou, did you say that Sharon was Polish?"

"Well, I don't know. Are you Polish, Sharon?"

"Actually," Sharon says, "My family did come from Poland, but I never heard about the sardine trick."

"Jeez", Louie says, "Polish. The truth is the Polacks don't get the credit they deserve. I bet if I ask you some questions you could change a lot of minds here tonight. How many people here think the Polacks are the smartest people in the world?"

The crowd responds as Louie knew they would, with good natured boos and cat calls.

"So you see, Sharon, you got a lot of work ahead of you. Okay, let's ask some questions. Sharon, do you know why elephants don't use Kotex?"

Before she has a chance to utter a sound, Louie yells, "Would you, if you had to change it with your nose?"

"I got a question." I say, "Do you know what Spanish Fly is?" Without waiting I answer, "It's a zipper, on a Spics pants."

"She knew that," Louie yells. "I could tell she knew that. She's very smart. I was talking to her before and she told me that a Women's monthly is a magazine."

"She is very smart," says Larry. "I know a Polish couple that's married forty five years, and they still play sex games."

"Get out of here," Lou tells Larry. "Forty five years? What do they do? Maybe Sharon could try it."

"Well Lou, when they go to bed they lie side by side, and then the wife reaches over and pulls the husbands schmuck straight up, and stretching it out, she lets it go. Then they watch and make bets on what side its going to fall on."

"It's always a problem when it falls," Lou quips.

"Only the Polacks would do that. They're smart, very smart. I once saw two drunken Polacks walking down a set of train tracks. The first one said, Jesus, this is the longest set of stairs that I've ever seen. And the second one said, it ain't the stairs that bother me, it's these low fucking handrails."

"What do you think, Sharon? Has being up here made you any smarter? Stay a while. We really want to ask you some questions."

Chapter 19

Here the bride comes

Sharon sipped the drink her sister had passed to her. Encouraged by Larry, she then handed it to him. Louie takes Sharon's hand and leads her off her stool for a moment, spinning her around for all to see.

"Very classy," he says, "a very good dresser. Look at that skirt. Is that the new mini-skirt that all the movie stars are wearing?"

"I think what she's wearing is called a jet skirt."

"Why's it called a jet skirt?"

"Because, it just about covers, the cockpit."

"You gotta be careful, Sharon, because sometimes, a dress like that can get you in trouble. I remember a girl who went to buy a pair of shoes, and she was wearing a skirt like yours. Every time the shoe clerk tried fitting her with shoes, she'd see him looking up her dress and mumbling to himself, 'Boy, I'd like to fill it up with ice cream and, eat it out.' She finally stormed out of the store and told her husband.

Sharon tugged on her mini and laughed. Expecting Louie to continue, she waited. Moments passed and the silence became awkward. Not knowing what to do, she asked, "So, what happened?"

Louie adjusted his guitar and quietly said, "Nothing. He did absolutely nothing. You see, Sharon, he figured any man who could eat that much ice cream, was too big for him to fuck with...so just be careful what you wear. You wouldn't want Hal to get beat up over your Pistachio, would you?"

"Man oh man, look at those legs."

"Hey look, everybody, Larry's awake. Welcome back. Every once in a while, he takes a nap."

"I'm surprised I dozed off. Legs like hers get my attention. I once knew a girl who had legs just like hers. I couldn't pry them apart, I mean, tell them apart. She was a pretty good dancer, too."

"What do you mean a pretty good dancer?"

"Well, it was very weird. You see, on her right leg, she could dance real well, but on her left leg, she wasn't too good. But I gotta say this, that between her two legs, that girl made a hell of a living."

"You have to be careful. I know a young couple, who were making out in the back seat of his car, and his girlfriend was wearing a mini-dress just like the one you're wearing. Suddenly, a cop showed up. The boy, seeing the cop, said, "Uh oh, fuzz." The girl looked up at him and said, "Hey, what'd you expect, a pony tail…I'm only fifteen."

"Hey Sharon," Larry whines, "Did you hear, what the Italian lady said when she was gang-banged in the back seat of a rented car? "Hey, that's a Hurts." I follow up before the laughter ends.

"This cop pulls up to a car wreck, and as he gets closer, he hears a man yelling, 'God damn these seatbelts…God damn these seatbelts.' The cop sticks his head in the car and says, 'Are you crazy, fella. Why that seatbelt probably saved your life. Your girlfriend went right through the windshield.' The man looks up at the cop, and says, 'I know, officer, but did you see what she has in her hand?'"

Louie strikes a cord on his guitar, and begins to sing,

"If the dresses get any shorter,
And, the girls get more brave,
there's gonna be one more place to powder,
and another place to shave,
And when it comes to remembering faces,
I'll never go to the head of the class,
But you, Bubbala, you I'll remember,
'cause I never forget an ass.

Without missing a beat, and while the crowd is still laughing, we sing,

East side, west side, all around the town,
They call her bareback Sharon,
'cause her pants are always down,
Now Sharon not Italian, so she's not crazy for pork,
 But she gets a lot a Sau-zech-ah
Onnnnn, the sidewalks, of New York.

The guitar, bass and snare drum change rhythm, and we start a song with an echo. Every line that Louie ends, we echo, sometimes more then once.

Is it true, (is it true)
what they say,(what they say)
about Sharon,
(Sharon, Sharon, Sharon)
Does she really have, a product to sell,
(Absolutely, it's already boxed,)
After years of pushin' 'n' pokin',
Sharon never turned down a pass,
Don't you think its mighty peculiar,
She's as tight as a clam shell,
(That rhymes with sell,)
Is it true, what they say, about Sharon,
(Sharon, Sharon, Sharon)
She never gets enough of that wonderful stuff, all night long,
(All night long)
Is she smart (Yeah) Is she good (Yeah)
Does she take care of the neighborhood,
(And Staten Island Too)
If its true, that's where I, belong,
 (Up in yours)
If it's true that's where I belong.

As the applause ends, Louie says, "I don't know if you caught it, but we mentioned the cops a few time. Why do you think we did that?"

"Because... you try to mention every body and everything?"

"No, because we have eight of New York's Finest here, and one of them is getting married, just like you. His name is Brian Kelly."

The bachelors go wild, standing and clapping.

"Now Sharon," Louie says, while putting on an Irish brogue, "Let me ask you, with a name like Brian Kelly, what do you think his heritage would be."

"Irish?"

"What a smart son-of-a-bitch she is. Doctor Nebwitz is getting some bargain. Tell me, did you ever go out with an Irishman?"

"Only once in High School."

"So you weren't serious?"

"No."

"It's a good thing you weren't. I knew an Irishman who married a Jew. When they had a baby, they called it a Micky-Mocky."

"It could be worse," Larry says, "I heard about a Spanish guy who married an Arab girl...They had a baby, so they called it a sparerib."

"I know an Irish guy who married an Italian girl, but it worked out okay. The Irishman liked the idea that the Italian girl could mash the potatoes with her feet."

"The best I've heard of was a young Puerto Rican couple who were about to make love for the first time. I step closer to the mic, and say, "She was four, and he was five. When they undressed, the little girl looked down at the boy, and pointing at his privates, she said in a slow Hispanic cadence, Pedro,oooooh, what is dat? Pedro answered, 'That is my rrrrr-rope. Then, looking a little lower, she asked, 'And Pedrooooo, what are those two things down there?' Pedro answered, 'These are my two nuts.' The little girl looked at him, and said, 'Pedrooooo, please... untie your two knots, and give me more rrrrrrrope."

"Seriously, Sharon, a young bride's best friend is usually her pharmacist, because they can teach you a lot about birth control. You know, years ago, the neighborhood drug store was a very important part of the community, because you could get just about anything at the drug store. They not only sold drugs, but they sold perfume and candy, and some even sold food. I remember once, I was waiting for a prescription to be filled, and a guy walked in and said to the druggist, 'Excuse me, but do you fit diaphragms? The druggist said, 'Sure we do.' The guy said, 'Great, then please wash your hands, and make me a cheese sandwich."

Without, hardly a pause, Louie continues, "But if I was a young bride like you, and wanted to know about birth control, I'd ask an

Italian. I knew an Italian girl who tried to keep her husband away by douching with garlic and oil. It didn't work. He'd just pop up his head and yell out, 'Hey, who made the salad? Who made the salad?"

"They love eating their tomatoes," says Larry. "I knew an Italian girl that used the rhythm method. You know, that's fifteen days on, and fifteen days off."

Louie says, "Wait a minute, isn't that called Rhythm and Blues?"

"No…It's rhythm and blows."

"Yeah, and another thing, those birth control pills don't really work," says Larry. "My wife tried them and every time she stood up, they fell out."

"Same thing with that foam they're advertising. I know an Italian mother who asked her daughter how she liked using the foam, and the daughter said, "It scares me, Ma. The first night we used it, I looked down at Angelo, and he looked like a mad dog."

"Yeah," I say, "That's why the best method is the bucket."

Sharon was giggling and through her laughter she asked, "The what?"

"Let me explain," I said. "I knew an old Italian mother, who was disappointed that her daughter didn't have any bambino's, so when the daughter said that she used the bucket, the mother looked as confused as you just did. The daughter explained, 'Mama, you know that I'm five foot five, and Gino is only four feet, eight inches tall, so we stand up when we make-a-da love. What we do is, when we make-a-da screw, I get Gino to stand on the bucket. And then, Mama, I look into his eyes. Mama, let me tell you, when his eyes get a little cloudy, and his hair gets a little curly, and his breath gets sucked in like this, Ah, ah ah… That's when I kick-a-da bucket."

"All this is very important, Sharon, but let me ask you a personal question. Do you ever pray?"

"Oh sure," she says. "Mostly I pray for good health and things like that."

"That's very wise," says Louie. "Do you think that Hal prays?"

"I'm not sure. Why do you ask?"

"I ask, because I knew a guy just like Hal, you know, a Jewish foot doctor…they're a dime a dozen these days….anyway, when his bride came out of the bathroom all dolled up for their first night together, she found him on his knees, praying. She asked, 'What are you praying for?' He answered that he was praying for guidance. She looked at him, and said, 'Why don't you worry about stiffness and hardness, and leave the guidance to me."

Sharon slaps her thighs and says, "That's a good one."

I say to Sharon, "I knew a guy named Harold Goldfarb who was a biology student at NYU, and one day he came home and said to his father, 'Hey Dad, can you help me out? I need three dollars for a guinea pig, and the father said, 'Here's five, get a nice Jewish girl."

"Hey Sharon, do you know why there are no Polish Pharmacist in New York. The reason you can't find any, is that they can't figure out how to get those tiny little bottles into the typewriter."

Louie says, "Sharon, we want to give you something to remember us by, for joining us on stage. Can you guess what it is?"

"I got no idea."

"I didn't think you would. Let me describe it. It can fit in your hand, (Yeah) and it's over a foot long, (Yeah) and it's as hard as a rock. Do you know what it is?

"Not if it's over a foot long, I don't."

"No, it's not that, it's just a bottle of Champagne. Thanks for helping us out, and have a great life. Let's have a big hand for Sharon."

As she leaves the stage Louie picks up his notes and says, "Let's see who else we got to work with?"

Chapter 20

When Irish eyes are tearing

"Are there any Irishmen here?"

The Irish make their presence known by yelling and clapping, helped along by the blast of an air horn. Louie scans his notes and says, "I don't think we've had eight cops in here, since Larry's sister got arrested for impersonating a circus performer. That's right. She claimed that she was the one that led the elephants down Fifth Avenue. Do you remember that Brian? For those who didn't see it, picture this. There are eight elephants marching, trunk to tail, trunk to tail, trunk to tail. Suddenly, the last one tripped…ripped out eight ass holes."

"His sister should have been on line…that would have made it nine."

Louie addresses the audience. "Brian Kelly has chosen to have his last fling, right here, at The Crazy Country Club. So, to honor him, why don't we look Irish?"

Reaching above us to the rafters, we each retrieve a green derby. Lou starts a beat. It's a soft beat, with a light snare drum and bass. It's a background for Louie. He says, "I love the Irish. Nobody throws a party like the Irish. Nobody drinks like the Irish."

I interrupt him. "I know a true story about an Irishman who went out partying, and after a lot of drinks and a few punches in the head, he ended up in the bathroom to take a leak. When he looked down to grab his schmuck, he saw two of them. When he went to grab the big one, the little one pissed on his shoe. That's a true story."

Larry says I got a true story. "An Irishman came home from work one day, and found his wife Gertie, standing in front of the mirror, stark naked, admiring herself. He looked his overweight wife up and down, and said, "What's wrong with you Gertie…are you daft?"

"Well," she answered, "I went to the doctor today, and he told me that, for a woman my age, I've got a beautiful body."

"He did, did he. Did he say anything about that big Irish ass of yours?"

"No, Michael," she answered. "Your name was never mentioned."

Louie smiles and begins to read from his sheet. "I see Brian Kelly is here tonight, with his dad and uncle. The funny thing about Irish music is that it makes you want to do the jig. Now I'm not talking about doing the black girl on Third Avenue, I'm talking about dancing. I can't figure it out. I play Italian Music and all I want to do is eat. Right now I'm not hungry, so let's dance."

The guitar starts an Irish Jig, and the place starts clapping along. We sing in harmony to the fast paced number. We dance to the beat, and when we look to the audience, they join in. With the help of the waiters clapping, the Club resembles an Irish pub. We start the song.

Oh, here's to the men of sixty and past,
Who lived their lives and lived them fast,
And here's to the girls of twenty and four,
Who sat on their laps and begged for more,
But all they could do was sit and tell her,
About what they would do as a young fella,
But now they can't do anything,
Their shillelagh's in a sling,

She takes the bad with the good,
The good with the best,
She does it for sport,
She does it for jest,
She'll try to get ten, but she'll take less,
Her box is the community chest.

Louie holds the last note as me and Larry sing,
'Shake it for uncle Mike me boy, and pull it for Sister Kate.

"I feel proud dressed up as an Irishman," Louie says, "with me green hat and all. It's like the Saint Paddy's Day Parade. I love watching the Irish march up Fifth Avenue, and then, stagger down Sixth. I remember last year when a young lass, tried streaking the parade by running across Fifth Avenue, completely nude."

I ask him,, "Well, tell us lad, what happened?"

Louie replies, "Well the Grand Marshall stopped her just in time. He told her she couldn't do it unless she was wearing some green."

Larry says, "So what happened, Laddy?"

"Well, she took a bunch of spinach, and shoved it in her crotch. She ran, but she never made it across the street."

"Did the Grand Marshall grab her?"

"No, before she got across, Popeye ate her."

Larry yells, "Well, blow me down."

I step up and say, "I got a true Irish story. One day Mrs. Murphy was at home, peeling her potatoes, when the doorbell rang. She opened it, and found Mr. Smith, the foreman from the local brewery where her husband worked, standing there, looking sad. He told her, 'Mrs. Murphy, I've got terrible news. Today, your dear husband Mike had a terrible accident. The poor man, while he was working, fell into a vat of beer, and I'm sorry to say, the poor lad drowned.

Oh, my God, Mrs. Murphy screamed, The poor man didn't stand a chance.

Oh yes he did, said Mr. Smith. You see, he came out twice, to piss."

Larry says, "Now that's a true Irishman. I wonder what clan he's in."

Louie says, "Hey. You must be confused, because I think you're thinking about a Scotsman. They're the ones who come from clans."

Larry says, "Hey, imagine if a Scotsman married an Italian...every night they could have clans and macaroni."

I say to Louie, "There's something wrong with Larry tonight. He should know that the Scots wear the kilts. The only problem is that, all the kilts look the same."

Louie says, "Not true. Addressing the audience in a confidential tone, he says, "There is one way to tell what clan a Scotsman comes from. You see, you just reach down and feel under his kilt. If you find a quarter-pounder, he's a Mac Donald."

Larry says, "Remember the commercial for Burger King?"

"Of course," we yell. Louie hits a chord and we all begin to sing.
"We'll hold your pickle if you let us,
weird positions don't upset us,
all we ask is that you let us,
do it our way."

"I think all of the Irish should wear kilts at the Saint Paddy's Day Parade. One year I was walking down Fifth Avenue and an drunken Irishman approached me and said, 'Excuse me, sir, but is my fly open? I looked and told him no, and he said, 'Well it should be, because I'm taking a leak."

Louie replies, "You can never tell about what an Irishman is going to do. I remember seeing two cops talking to a drunk, and the drunk was holding a set of keys in his hand. The cops said, "What are you doing standing in the middle of the street?"

The drunk looked down at his keys, and said, "Jesus Christ, somebody stole me car."

The cops looked at each other and then said, "Well, we've got to take you in to see the judge, but before we do, you'd better clean yourself up, and whatever else you do, you'd better close your fly."

The drunk once again looked down, and said, "Oh shit, they stole me girl too."

Louie hits a chord and says, "I've got a true Irish story. There was this Irishman who was in New York for the first time, and while sightseeing, he gets lost. He realizes that he's got to go to the men's room, but in looking around he sees only factories. Becoming desperate, he tries a door and it opens. He walks down this long corridor searching for a place to relieve him self. He yells, "Is there anyone here?"

Just then, some colored lady sticks her head out of a room and says...

Larry interrupts. "Wait a minute, Lou...what did you just say?"

Louie begins, "I just said this colored lady...

Larry again stops him. "No good. You can't say that anymore. They don't want to be called 'Colored,' they want to be called Black."

Louie answers by questioning, "Are you sure? If you call them Black, they'll kick the shit out of ya. I always called them Colored."

Larry insists, "That's the way they want it. They're Black, and that's that."

I joins in by saying, "I'm not so sure about that. Just think about it. There's Vida Blue, and Lou repeats, "Yeah, Vida Blue. There's Mean Joe Green, and Lou repeats, Yeah, mean Joe Green. There's Slappy White and there's Red Fox, and....

Larry stops us by screaming, "Okay, you're right...fuck them... they're Colored, they're Colored. Now finish your story?"

I tell Louie, "Now take it from the Colored lady."

"Okay. So the Irishman yells out, 'Quick, quick, I need a lavatory.' The cleaning lady, doesn't understand him, and says, 'A laboratory? Why shit, that's down the hall, third door on the right.'

The Irishman runs down the hall and opens the door. Looking in, he sees it's not a lavatory, but a laboratory. There are all kinds of jars and glass canisters filled with bubbling liquids, but the Irishman thinks, 'When you got to go, you've got to go. So, in desperation, he just grabs the jar closest to him and starts to pee in it. With that, there's a terrible explosion. The Colored women runs into the room, and screams, "Oh my God, Look at your legs…Oh my God, look at your arms…Oh my God, look at your chest.

The Irishman yells out, "Forget about those parts…look for me hand…it's got me cock in it."

As the crowd settles down, Louie tells them that that isn't the first time he heard a story about Irishman and Colored people. Adjusting his guitar he smiles at the Kelly table and says, "Hey, do you remember that story about the merchant marine ship that went down and a few of them made it to shore where they were captured by Cannibals? Well, this is a true story, Brian, and let me tell you what happened. The Chief cannibal said to the first sailor, 'Where you from', and the sailor said, England and the chief said, Throw him in the pot. The second sailor said he was from Poland and the chief said, throw him in the pot. When the third sailor was questioned he said he was from Ireland and the chief said, let him go. Another cannibal questioned why the chief was letting him go, because he looked good enough to eat, and the chief said, 'Naw, let him go. The last Irishman we threw in the pot ate all the fucking potatoes.' "

As the audience settles down, Louie returns to his notes, and reads, "Brian Kelly is marrying a Greek girl. It says here that she's a nice girl, and that her brothers are here. You can immediately tell which ones are her brothers."

"You mean to tell me, that you can look at that table of guys, and tell which ones are her brothers?"

"Absolutely, positively. Just look at those guys. The two who are smiling the most, that's her brothers. And, let's face it, why shouldn't they smile? After all, once she gets married, they'll have the whole fucking bed to themselves."

"It says here that they were raised in Greece. Everybody knows that the Greeks are nice people. Of course, they've got their own way of doing things, like when it comes to making love. In my book, they seem to miss by an inch."

Larry yells, "That reminds me of a Greek who went golfing. After ten minutes of play, he burst into the Clubhouse screaming for a doctor. A man says, "I'm a doctor, what's wrong?" The Greek says, "It's my wife. She's been hit with a golf ball." The Doctor says, "Really. Where'd she get hit?" The Greek says, "Right between the first and second hole." The doctor looks around and says, "Between the first and second hole. Shit! That doesn't give me much room to operate, does it?"

Louie says, "I love the Greeks and I love their wedding song." He strums, as we sing,

"I'm walking behind you, on your wedding day..."

Larry says, "You can always tell when a Greek makes a comeback... His ass is all wet."

"I have a friend, who's Greek, and I remember his wedding song," Louie says. He does the introduction to the love song, *Second Time Around.* Instead we sing,

Love is lovelier, the
other way around,
With, your back to me,
doing pushups, on the ground.
Who can say what miracles,

are brought up from the past,
There are those, I bet,
Who come but once, and yet,
I'm oh, so glad we met,
the other way around.

Louie picks up the beat, saying, "Do you remember the Italian wedding song?" We're in full rhythm when we begin to sing, a parody to the popular commercial,

"Get a Hart's Collar, a three and one collar…"

"I love Italian ballads, I say. Do you remember this one?"

Louie strums a long drawn out introduction to the Connie Frances hit, Mama. We sing it this way.

"Mama………. How come Papa's got come on his pajama?"

"Do you remember this one?

Ve do mardi quande bella,
Your Trojan tastes like mozzarella….

Larry stands front stage pulling on a condom that he's bitten. The music fades out as Larry says, "How about the Lesbians? They got a wedding song too."

With no hesitation, we sing,

"YES, we have no bananas, we have no bananas today"…again we fade out.

Lou says, "Hey Larry, whatever you do, don't do anything to the Lesbians. In all my years associated with Lesbians, I've never gotten a lick of trouble from one of them."

"Lesbians look like regular girls," I say.

"Except, that they're sadder then regular girls," says Larry.

"Is that because they don't have boy friends," I ask.

"No," Lou answers. "It's because her vibrator is broken. Just like this girl sitting with this guy. He don't know it yet, but she's a lesbian."

"And you think her vibrator is broken?"

"With out a doubt."

"Hey sweetheart," Larry says, "when you get it fixed, you want to give me a buzz?"

I tell the girl, "I went out with a Lesbian once, and she looked just like you. As the night wore on, I got to the point where I wanted to get closer to this girl, so being slick in my manner, 'I said, "I got a great erection here. What do you think I should do with it?"

She looked at me very seriously, and said, "Now that you got the wrinkles out, I think you better wash it."

"My cousin had both the hiccups and an erection, at the same time. It was terrible. Every time he jerked, it jerked back."

"When you said, 'Jerk', I thought you said, 'McGirk.' You've heard of killer McGirk, haven't you? He's the toughest Irish wrestler in the world, known for his famous 'Ferocious Pretzel Hold.' It seems that whenever he got someone in the Ferocious Pretzel Hold, they never get out. That's the way it was, until he met Killer Kowalski. What a match."

"Leave it to a Polack to figure out that Pretzel Hold."

"What happened, Lou? Did Kowalski get beaten too?"

"Not, exactly. Here's what happened. The two men came out to the center of the ring, and within a moment, they clashed. Immediately, McGirk got Kowalski into his Ferocious Pretzel Hold, but with only a few seconds left before blacking out, Kowalski suddenly threw McGirk into the air and pinned him. When the reporters surrounded Kowalski at the press conference, they wanted to know how he broke free. Kowalski described it like this.

When I realized I was in the Ferocious Pretzel Hold, I knew I had only seconds before I'd black out. I looked up and saw these two things hanging in front of my face. In desperation, I reached out and bit them. Boy, I'll tell ya something. You'd be surprised at the strength you get when you bite your own balls."

"Hey Brian, there's a lot you can learn from balls. When I was going on my honeymoon, my doctor recommended that I bring along a honeymoon ball kit. I asked him what that was, and he said, 'It's red paint and green paint, a brush and a hammer.' Here's what you do. You paint one ball red, and the other ball green. If your bride looks down and says, 'That's the funniest pair of balls I've ever seen,' you hit her with the fucking hammer."

"Look, Brian's laughing," says Louie.

"One thing about the Irish…they got the greatest sense of humor in the world. And I knew another guy, also named Brian, who said to his bride–to–be, Honey, on our honeymoon night, instead of just jumping into the sack, and making love all night, I'm going to utilize my Irish sense of humor and make you laugh. So, on the honeymoon night that's what he did. Reaching down, he grabbed his crotch and said, MAKE A WISH,SWEETHEART, MAKE A WISH.

His bride, looked down at him and said, I know that I'm not Irish but I want to show you that we Greeks have a sense of humor too. You want me to make a wish…OK, here's my wish."

Going into a parody of an old song, entitled, I want a girl, just like the girl, that married dear old dad, Louie strikes a chord and we begin to sing, as Louie says, "And here's what the Greek girl said,

I wish you had a dong (Ding dong)
Just like the dong,
That hangs from your best man,
He never got that tool,(No,No)
From what he learned in school,
It was made by hand,
A real old fashioned dong,
So round, so firm,
You better have a sense of humor,Brian,
Because, you got such a little fucking worm,
Oh, I want a dong, just like the dong,
That hangs from your best man.

The place goes crazy. The Kelly party screams and slaps Brian on the back, teasing him. Louie addresses Brian and thanks him for coming in and sharing a little of his private life. He then asks Brian if he ever served in the Army. Brian answers that he hasn't, but that he takes his hat off to them, for what they do. Louie says, "And that's what we're going to do. We're going to take off our Irish hats, and do a salute to them. Quick, let's look Military, let's look rough and tough."

All three of us stretch forward and into the rafters reaching for a new hat.

Chapter 21

Veterans and Nurses

Louie points to the two Rangers and says, "Now that's what I call health care. Two beautiful nurses taking care of two of our boys in uniform. You guys are in good hands."

"And good legs too."

"Now you've done it Larry, you've gone and said the magic word."

"What do you mean the magic word?"

"You know that every night we have a magic word. Tonight, the word is legs."

"Oh, that's right, and tonight I want to spread the word, spread the word."

"Why do I even talk to you? I'm better off just reading my notes." Lou turns his back to Larry, and says, "Tonight, we're in good company. These two Army Rangers, Augie Pastore and Jimmy Patch, are both here recuperating at The Veterans Hospital, from wounds that they received fighting in Viet Nam. We know what it's like to be away from your family for a long time. We realize that it takes time to get back on track. So be patient boys. Let them nurse you back to health."

"That's right. You're home now. Everything's going to be fine. Take one problem at a time."

"I think," says Larry, "That the biggest problem is the lack of sex. If the Army could develop a K-ration for sex, they'd solve a lot of problems."

"Yeah," I say, "Like a box in a box."

Larry says, "You might have something there. I remember my cousin JoJo. He was away during the Korean War for about two years, and of course, he had no sex. Korea was cold and barren, just like Louie's wife. Anyway, JoJo requested an emergency leave, so he could go home and satisfy his cravings. His Captain didn't understand, so he denied him. He told JoJo, 'Why would anyone want to go home to have sex. Hey, we have it all here. Think about it. We have Wacs, we have Wav's, we have nurses and we have Orientals. Why would anyone want to go home just to get laid?'"

JoJo looked his Officer straight in the eye, and said, 'Listen Captain, believe me when I say, that I've whacked it, and I've waved it, I've nursed it, and I've orientated it. Don't you think it's about time I took it home, and gave it an Honorable Discharge."

"I think your right." I take a drink of my scotch, as I say, "It's so important to do that. My uncle was away for a long time, too.

"Korea?"

"No. Sing Sing. He called up my aunt from the train station, and said, "Honey, if you want to be the first one I make love to, make sure your mother doesn't answer the door. Well, lucky for her mother, my aunt was waiting at the door, and he immediately attacked her with his pent up passion. After about a minute of doing it to her, he suddenly stopped, and said, 'Honey, what's going on? While I was away, did you learn a new trick?"

"What are you talking about? I didn't learn anything new."

"Well," he screamed, "I don't understand. Every time I push in, your toes curl up."

His wife said, "What's wrong with you? That's not a trick, you Schmuck. You didn't give me enough time to get my panty hose off."

Louie laughs. Its infectious sound is louder then the joke demands, but carries the audience with him. He announces, "Jimmy Patch, a Ranger for two years. Tell me Patch, are all the Rangers paratroopers?"

Patch says, "Its part of the training. You have to get your wings."

"I see. You know, Patch, years ago, there weren't any Black paratroopers in the Army. Segregation was still practiced during the Second World War, and it wasn't until the Korean War that the rules changed. I remember reading about the first Black paratrooper. I don't like thinking back to those dark days, but that's the way things used to be. Anyway, here's what happened.

When the first Black volunteer for the Rangers showed up, he was taken without any training, into an airplane for his first jump. The sergeant, who was an old red-headed rebel, ordered him to stand up in the doorway and prepare to jump. When Private Elroy Jones protested, saying that he didn't have on a parachute, the sergeant told him this.

In the Rangers, we're rough and tough. We don't use parachutes. What we do is, we jump out and then we flap our arms real fast, just like a bird, and when we're three feet from the ground, we yell Geronimo. That's how we do it."

Elroy, who badly wanted to become a Ranger, jumped. The sergeant closed the plane door, and began to laugh, realizing that the man had actually jumped without a parachute. About three minutes had passed, when suddenly the sergeant heard banging on the door. Not knowing what to think, he opened the planes door, and there, flapping his arms like wings, was Elroy. "Hey Sarge," Elroy screamed, "What was the name of that Guinea again?"

"I thought only the Army's Green Berets jumped without chutes," I tell him.

Louie answers, "Well, there are lots of specialized units through out the world. You know, Italy has a real tough Army. Maybe you've heard of them. In Italy, they are called, The Yellow Beret. In Italian, it's, Il cappelo giallo."

"Wow. That sounds tough."

"And since then, the Italians have changed their uniforms. Before they specialized, they used to wear Kilts and sneakers. This way, they could run and shit at the same time. Before we sing their fighting song, first, let's look like the Italian Army."

Again we reach into the rafters above, and pull down our Yellow Berets. The guitar does a slow walk around the notes and everyone recognizes the Green Beret melody. The snare drum is beating and the bass is plucking as Lou begins the song. We echo every thing he sings.

Dirty feet, (dirty feet) hairy chest,(Hairy chest)
One hundred wops, (one hundred wops)
Italy's best, (Italy's best)
While the others fight,(While the others fight)
We shout hooray, (yelling, Hooray, go ahead and kill each other, we don't care, just leave us alone…)
Courageous wops, (courageous wops)
in their Yellow Beret.
Yellow Beret, (Yellow Beret)
And, jock to match, (jock to match)
I fight for peace, (I fight for peace)
A piece of snatch, (A piece of snatch)
One hundred wops, (one hundred wops)
they're gonna test today, (gonna test today)
Sixty nine, (sixty nine)
Will blow away, (will blow away)

March, march, march, march….
We marches in a slow circle as the crowd claps in time. We continue
the song.
March all day, (March all day)
Looking for, (looking for)
Contraceptives,(Contraceptives)
In a drug store, (In a drug store)
But everybody's closed, (But everybody's closed)
It's a holiday, (It's a holiday)
The Italians use,(What do they use)
(Baggies?) No. They use their yellow Beret.

"Hey," Larry yells," I don't think Augie Pastore liked that song. I think he was bored."
"What makes you say that Larry?"
"Well, I think his ass just fell asleep."
"That's ridiculous," says Louie. "What makes you say that?"
"I think I just heard it snore."
"Yeah, well, I don't think that his nurse heard it.
I think she's a deaf mute."

"Why do you say that, Lou?"

"Because, I thought that Augie was feeling her up, but it seems he's only talking to her…and, I'll tell you something, fellas, the way he's talking to her, no one can get a finger in edgewise."

"Yeah. You'd have to pray for an opening."

"Praying, don't solve every problem. Last week I walked into church, and there was a young girl, standing there, washing her hands with Holy water. Her girlfriend asked her what she was doing, and she said, "I told the priest in confession, that I'd touched my boyfriend's thing, and he said, to wash my hands in Holy water."

"Oh, shit," the second girl muttered. "You better save me some…I think I have to gargle."

"Did you say that your uncle came home from Sing Sing by train?"

"That's right. I think he rode in the Pullman car."

"I don't like trains. They're too uncomfortable. I have a cousin who was traveling on an overnight trip, and went to sleep in an upper berth. There was a beautiful girl occupying the berth below him. During the night, my cousins toupee' fell off his head, and somehow fell between the bed and the wall. When he woke up with the breeze, he became frantic. He searched every where with no luck. He concluded that it had fallen to the bunk below. So very quietly, he squeezed his hand along the wall to the bunk below, and started feeling around.

The girl below woke up, and noticed his hand stretching towards her. Feeling horny, she began to maneuver her body to better help my cousin. When he'd reach to the right, she'd move to the right. When he'd go to the left, she'd move to the left. Finally, when the magic moment happened, and his hand landed on her privates, she yelled out, 'That's it, that's it!' That's when my cousin screamed back, "Oh no it's not, lady. You see, I part mine on the side."

Louie again goes to his notes. "I can tell by his name, that Augie is Italian. I'm not quite sure what Patch is."

"I bet he's a country boy," says Larry.

"Yeah," I say. "He told me he was from Texas."

"Do you remember the story about the toughest bar in Texas. It made all the papers. A reporter, from the Daily News was there, and wrote about it. It seems that as the reporter was watching, a young cowboy told the barmaid, 'Barmaid, I'm from Kentucky, and we're rough and ready in Kentucky.' With that said, he held up his middle finger and said, 'Barmaid, shoot it off." The barmaid, without flinching, drew her pistol and shot it off. Another man, stood up and told the barmaid that he was from Georgia, and holding up two fingers, he said, barmaid, shoot them both off. She did as he asked, and shot them both off. Now, sitting in the corner of the room, sat a little Jewish man from New York. Quietly sipping his Seltzer, he watched the whole thing. As the reporter observed, the Jew, not to be outdone by the cowboys, approached the barmaid with the smoking pistol. Suddenly, he jumped up on the bar, and dropped his pants. With his pecker fully exposed, he looked down at the barmaid. She asked what he wanted her to do. He answered, "Vel, were rough and tough in New York too."

"So," the barmaid said, "Do you all want me to shoot it off, too?"

"Nah!" the Jew replied. "Just kiss it a little...it'll shoot off by itself."

"I love the South," Lou says. "I was at a southern ball and asked a lady, if she knew the Minuet. She looked me straight in the eye and told me, "No honey. I don't even remember the men I laid."

"Hey," I say to the soldiers, "Were you guys drafted?"

Augie hollered that they both enlisted for the Rangers.

"They enlisted," Louie replies, "They're true American heroes. Some guys ran to Canada, while others did their best hiding out at home. But not these two, they stepped up like men."

"There was a story going around," I say, "about a guy who was dodging the draft. He was being chased down a street, trying to avoid capture by the military police closing in. Suddenly, the draft-dodger found himself in front of a Catholic Convent. Desperate, he banged on the door. When a Nun answered, he pleaded for her to hide him. He screamed, "Please sister, I don't want to go to Viet Nam, I don't want to go to Viet Nam."

The Nun, knowing that if they caught the deserter, they would execute him, told the man to hide under her Habit. She had no sooner closed the Convent door, when the MP's showed up. They banged on the door, and inquired if she had seen the draft-dodger. She said that she hadn't seen anyone, and they left. She then, in a calm and sweet voice, told the young man that he could come out from under her Habit. When he did, he thanked her profusely for having saved his life. Then, as if he had had a revelation, he said to the Nun, "You know Sister, it's odd the way we met. I'm not Catholic, and so I've often wondered what you Nuns wore under your Habit. By the way, Sister, what were those two things balanced on my right shoulder."

The Nun looked quickly to the right and left, and said, "Shut up, you stupid bastard. I don't want to go to Viet Nam either."

A young college kid boo's the joke, and yells, "Hell no, we wont go."

The audience reacts and boos the college kid, who seems to be alone in his opinion. Louie steps closer to the microphone.

"I didn't realize that we had one here tonight. But looking at him, it's hard to tell what he is. Could it be that he's just a schmuck?"

"Hey Lou, what we need is a qualified opinion. Sharon Levine went to college. Maybe she knows what he is."

Lou says, "That's true. Why didn't I think of It. Tell me Sharon, would you say that this college boy is a regular schmuck or a real schmuck?"

Sharon finds herself back in the Show, and laughing she says, "I don't know?"

"She looks confused," says Larry. "Maybe she doesn't know the difference."

"You would think," I say, "That any Jewish girl would know a Schmuck when she sees it. Maybe we'll have to help her out."

"All right, Sharon. Now listen carefully. We've looked him over and we don't think that he's a regular Schmuck. To us he looks like a real Schmuck. Do you know what a real schmuck is? A real Schmuck is a guy who gets out of the shower to take a leak. That's a real schmuck."

I say, "He kind of looks like a real Schmuck, but then again, Sharon, he might just be, a rat bastard. Do you know what a rat bastard is? That's a guy who runs away with your wife, and then brings her back."

Lou quickly says, "He might just be a loser. You know, that's a guy who has a wet dream and wakes up with the clap."

"When you think about it, he's just a college kid, and if anyone deserves some praise, it's our young people. How about, we do a little song for our pal, here."

The guitar starts the familiar melody of an old song called, *'Heartaches.'* It's sung in unison, like a sing-a-long, with the waiters asking everyone to join in. Of course, initially, the audience doesn't know the words, but catches on as we sing. They gladly add to the destruction of the heckler. We sing.

Hard on, hard on,
Why must we always deal with hard-on's,
We thought that you were a nice person,
But now we're through because you got me cursing you

Hard on, hard on,
And on your head we'll make a fart on,
In other places you're such a little dear,
Why must you be a hard on here.

The audience reacts with tremendous clapping. The college kid takes it on the chin and shuts up. Louie approaches the microphone and says, "Personally, I've had enough of hard-on's. I think I'd rather move on to something soft, like maybe a Playboy Bunny."

Larry yells out, "I've got a question. Are bunnies and rabbits the same thing?"

"What a question," Louie says. "What makes you ask something like that?"

"Because when I was a kid and went to camp, my troop leader gave us a tongue-twister. He wanted us to say, 'Richard and Robert raped the rabbit in the Rectum?" He knew one of the kids was Chinese, and would have a problem with pronouncing the letter R. But little Bing-bang-boom Chan, outsmarted the leader. He thought for a minute and answered, 'Dick and Bob banged the bunny in the bottom."

"There's no one smarter than a Chinaman. I think I once had a 'Bottom of the Bunny' in a Chinese restaurant. Yeah, I think I ordered a Number Two."

"What ever you did in a Chinese restaurant has nothing to do with our Bunny. Tonight, we have no number Two's, only, number One. What do you say, guys, do you see the difference?"

"What am I blind?"

"Why don't we get her to hop up here with us. Come on up, Jill. We got some questions."

Larry, who's all smiles, says. "Why don't I just dangle my carrot? Bunnies love carrots."

"Let's get her up here, first, and then we'll talk about your ever dangling carrot. It's been said that Bunnies laugh at the tiniest things, so maybe your schmuck stands a chance."

As she rises from her chair, the place goes wild. Louie announces, "Here's Jill, our own little Play boy Bunny, who came all the way from New Jersey to be here. Even though there's a river separating New York from New Jersey, all I can say is, that tonight, I'm happy to see that you came across. I hope you're from Freehold. Let's get her up here and see what we can learn about Bunnies."

Chapter 22

The Bunny Hop

As she makes her way to the stage, we do a little stripper music, and the waiters make cat calls as she passes them. As she walks the Bass drum keeps time, and every step is something to see. She attempts to make the big step up onto the stage but her shirt is short and too revealing. Louie tells Larry to help her up. Larry says he'd rather help her go down than go up. He steps down, picks her up and places her safely on stage. Jill stands to the cheers of the crowd, and purposely jiggles for effect.

Louie smile's, and welcome's her.

"You know you can trust us to treat you right, so don't be nervous. First of all, let me say, that Jill, we're so glad you came…before you got here…'cause we got lots to learn from you. For instance, we've heard that Bunny School, unlike Larry, is very hard, and that there's much to learn about the animal kingdom. For instance, we just learned what the elephant said when he sat on the Bunny. 'Hey,' he said, 'How'd I get that hare up my ass?' You probably knew that. We didn't, because we're from Brooklyn, so we don't know much about animals, except maybe for a few of our neighbors like Mike the Bear, Joey the Snake and Bruce The Moose.

First of all, let me say that you're absolutely gorgeous. I love the way you dress; tight sweater, mini skirt."

Larry interrupts. "Hey Lou, that's not a mini skirt. That's a turtle skirt."

"Oh," Louie says, "I didn't realize that you were an expert on women's clothing. You mean it's made from the shell of a turtle?"

"No. I mean, that it's worn two inches from the snapper."

Pointing to her hair, I say, "And I love her hair. It's blond and short, and probably easy to manage."

"I'm with you. I don't like long hair, either."

"Jill," says Louie," Did this ever happen to you? Like when you're driving down the street, did you ever stop for a red light, and the girl driving in front of you, is fluffing up her hair? I hate when they do that. I don't know why they do it, but girls with long hair are always fluffing up their hair."

Louie pauses for a moment, as I look Jill in the face and say, "Hey Lou, I know why they do that. The reason they're always fluffing up their hair, is because, they've got no balls to scratch."

Jill laughs when I say, "That's right. I've seen guys sitting in their cars for three light changes. Personally, the blinking yellows are my favorite."

Larry makes like he's steering a car with one hand and with the other he scratches himself, saying over and over, "Coffee and cake, coffee and cake. I love those coffee and cake lights."

Louie says, under his breathe, "You look like you've had too much coffee and cake."

"And Louie, "I say, looking Jill up and down, "You mentioned the way she dresses. You're right. Just look at her blouse. I'm pretty sure it's seersucker."

"What are you, a cloths expert too?"

"Nah, I'm no expert. But I'll tell ya something, if you look real close, you can see her suckers right through it."

Sal opens the door and let's in four people. Afraid that they'll attract attention, they stand at the bar. Louie looks at them, and then turns to Larry.

"Jeez, Larry, I thought for a minute that I was seeing double. If it wasn't for the mustache, I would have sworn that I was looking at your wife's brother."

Larry says, "What are ya blind? That guy doesn't have a mustache."

"Oh, I know he doesn't have a mustache…It's your wife that has the mustache."

"I can't argue that one. Although," Larry says, "That girl's built just like my wife…same boobs and everything."

"What are ya talking about? I wish you'd make up your mind. Last night she came here without tits, and you said, she looked like your wife. Tonight, she's wearing tits, and again, you say she looks like your wife. Make up your mind, will ya, make up your mind."

"I'm sorry Lou. I'm just a sucker for those things. I'll tell you something right now. If any of you guys make fun of my wife again, I'll eat the whole room."

I tell Larry that "I'm going to sit out there."

Louie says, "You're gonna eat the whole room? There's a lot of people out there, Larry, so I better help you out."

"Okay," says Larry. "You take the guys."

"Why not," chuckles Louie, "There's more to eat."

"Jill. Do you see what I got to put up with? I can't get answers from them, so I've got to ask you. Let me ask you this. Do you know how a Jewish girl makes a diaphragm? No! Well, here's what they do. They take a Spalding pink ball, and they cut it in half. Now they have two, one for their girlfriend."

"My sister used a pimple ball."

"John, your sister should have used a basketball. This way she could dribble before she shoots."

"His sister can handle two balls at the same time," says Larry.

"Hey Jill," says Lou. "Do you know anything about Frenchman? Well, did you hear about the Frenchman who married a Chinese girl. What a deal he made. You see, every night she sucked his shirt."

"Do you know anything about fish?"

Jill says that she knows how to order it. Not much else. Louie tells her there's a lot to know, like, did you hear about the Italian lady that went into a fish store, and said, "I wanna get some a fish." The clerk asked, "Fillet?" She answered, "No, for eat."

"I heard that, I heard that. Did you hear about the Italian lady who went into a deli, and said, "I wanna get summa beer."

The clerk said, "Anheuser Busch?" And she answered, "Nice, and how'sa yours?"

"Never mind the beer. Did you hear about Cott's soda and Cool cigarettes? They've merged. They call their new company, Cotts'n'Cool."

"That sells well in Little Italy."

"There's a new one that just came out. Did you hear about Black and Decker?"

Jill laughs and says that she didn't. "Well," Larry says, "They just merged with United Fruit, and their new product is a battery operated black banana that vibrates."

"That'll sell well in Little Italy too. They could use it to stir the sauce."

"Unbelievable," yells Louie. "And, what about all the Dolls, that are coming out, this year. Some of them look just like Jill. For instance, there's the Puerto Rican doll. Yeah, you wind it up, and it stabs your cousin."

"And what about the Italian doll," I yell out. "You wind it up, and it bangs your sister."

"I think your sister would sell well in Little Italy, too."

"Speaking of my sister, I recently went out and bought her a doll for her birthday."

Lou inquires, "Did you get her the Italian doll?"

"Nah, I got her the newest one out. I got her the Polish doll? You know, you just wind it up, and the poor fucking thing gets lost."

Lou strums a few chords, and then steps back. "You know, Jill, you're probably under the impression that we only work here. It's not true. We do other jobs, like, Anniversaries, Wedding's, Birthday parties…we do a lot of affairs. Why last week, we even did a Bris. Hey, we didn't mind. After all, it was no skin off our noses."

"Yeah. Remember Lou? Last month we did that Lesbian party. They seemed happy with us."

"That's right. But the best one was the gig we did in England. We did an all boys convention in London. I think it was in Prick-a-dilly Square. That's the only job I can think of that didn't turn out so great."

"Well, yes, but that wasn't our fault. You see Jill, they were very disappointed when they found out, that Big Ben was only a clock."

"True, but then they cheered up when they heard that Peter Sellers, was a male prostitute."

"Yeah, but they all agreed that Big Ben would have been a tough one to swallow."

"I'll munch on that. You know, I knew a fag who went to the doctor's, and when he got alone with the doctor, he whipped out his thing. He looked at the doctor and said, "Doc, look at this!" The doctor looked and said, "I don't see anything wrong with that." And the fag said, "I know…ain't it a beauty."

"You know, Jill, I don't think there's anything wrong with loving another man. It shouldn't be against the law."

"Hey Lou, speak for yourself. Personally, making love to a man leaves a bad taste in my mouth."

"Why don't we get off the fags? I feel like I'm doing two to five in Sing Sing."

"Two to five sounds more like, your, before and after pecker size."

"I know. I hate to brag."

"By all means, keep it to yourself."

"There's nothing wrong with being small. My sister, don't like anything small. Last month she went out and had her ovaries vaccinated."

"Why would anyone do that?"

"She said it prevents her from getting small cocks."

"All right Jill, now, that we've worked our way down to small cocks, I don't want you to lose interest, so why don't we do a song."

Lou begins an easy strum, and as he does, he tells Jill that he wants to dedicate this tune to all the Bunnies of the world. This is a true story, about another girl who had some great tail. Louie begins to sing,

I was making love to, Minnie the Mermaid,
Down at the bottom of the sea,
When I pet her, she shakes her tail,
When we're together, she's just like any other girl, I was making love to
Minnie the Mermaid,
Down at the bottom of the sea,

She's got the biggest pair of gills you've ever seen,
You should see her devour my little ole sardine,
Oh! I was making love, to Minnie the Mermaid,
Down at the bottom of the sea,

When Minnie squeezes me, by the rocks,
I don't know what's cooking', I go crazy looking,
Where does she keep her box?
Oh! I was making love to, Minnie the Mermaid,
Down at the bottom of the sea.

She puts her ball bearing, in my sex drive,
She can take a pickled Herring, and c'mon, c'mon, come alive,
I was making love to Minnie the Mermaid,
She thinks an awful lot of me,
We have to resort to sodomy,
Because she's got no bottom you see,
Now you may think I'm a bounder,
But I would never bang a flounder,
Minnie is the Mermaid, (Yeah, yeah)
Minnie is the Mermaid,
Minnie made a Baccala', out of me.

Lou laughs as Jill claps her hands, and adjusts her skirt. "Well, Jill, it was great having you up here, but then again, it would be great having you anywhere. But I think it's time to send you back to your friends."

"Hey Lou," Larry asks. "What do they call a bunch of Bunnies? Is it a Flock? Is it a Pride? Maybe it's a tribe."

"It's certainly not a tribe. Are you talking about a tribe in Africa or a tribe of Indians? I ask that because they're very different. For instance, do you know what the darkest spot in Africa is? It's looking up a Mau-Mau's Moo-moo."

"Now that's dark. Did you hear about the Black couple that went to Disney World and found themselves in front of a magic mirror. The women took the mirror and said,' Mirror, mirror, on the wall, make

151

my breasts as wide as I'm tall.' Poof! Suddenly she has size 54 breasts. The man sees this and takes the mirror into the bathroom and hangs it on the door. He says, Mirror, mirror, on the door, make my schmuck touch he floor. And POOF! When he looked down his fucking legs were gone."

"Did you hear what the Mau-Mau said, when he got Diarrhea? He said, Oh shit…I is melting."

"Okay, we better stop before we get carried away with Indians and natives."

"Indian chief say to squaw, 'Squaw, bring me drum' and the squaw says, Chief you want war drum…and the chief says, not war drum, me want cundrum…me want piece.."

"Hey, do you know how to tell a fag Indian? No, well he's the one who has scalps with handles."

Once again, we want to thank Jill for coming up here while we made fools of ourselves. A nice bottle of Champagne is waiting for you, as well as a hundred guys. You're a real sweetheart. Thanks honey."

The applause is long and loud as she makes her way to her seat. Louie grabs another slip of paper, and says, "Uh oh…Guess who's having another birthday?"

Chapter 23

To Smell A Rose

Mary Lombardo sat at the bar. As usual she looked great, younger than her eighty years. More than anything else she looked feminine. In contrast to her looks was a mouth that any truck driver would approve of. She was both sweet and spicy.

Her son Gus had first taken her to the Club on her seventy-fifth birthday. Since then, she'd turned her birthday into a yearly visit. She's a saucy old broad who'd been raised on hard times, and little money. She'd always retained her sense of blue humor, and loved the Club. She loved all the guys, and what they did. She'd surprised Louie a few times, by bringing her own birthday cake. One year it read, 'Old pots make the best soup.' Another year was, 'To Mary with the Hairy Canary.' She always sat at the bar, with Gus at her side. Gus enjoyed his Mom and her feisty ways. Everybody liked her.

As Louie begins strumming, we add rhythm.

"Holy shit, Mary, has another year passed? I can't believe it. Ladies and gentleman, sitting at the bar, in her usual seat, is the one, the only, Mary Lombardo. This sweetheart started celebrating five years ago, and hasn't sobered up yet. Mary has made the big turn, and is in fact, eighty years young today. I'd be remiss if I didn't thank her son Gus, for bringing his Mom tonight. I look at Mary, and I think, 'Look at the condition that she's in.' She's neat and trim, and I have to say, that for a women her age, she dresses beautifully."

"Yeah, and fast too!"

"Don't pick on her, Larry. Mary puts a lot of effort into staying healthy. When it comes to food, she's like a Dick-less Tracey. All of her boy friends claim, that she's almost a vegetarian, in that when they're together, she eats nuts, and then leaves."

"I believe it. Last week she began eating a very healthy breakfast. Every morning she has Rice Crispiest with Milk of Magnesia."

I say, "Hey, that sounds good. I'm going to try it."

"Be careful John. Twice last week, she snapped, crackled and shit. So be careful."

"Hey, it must be tough for Gus to get his Mom a birthday gift. After a while, you just run out of ideas."

"Gus came up with a winner last year. He got his mother a combination washer-dryer."

"Wow. A combination washer-dryer! That must have cost him a fortune."

"Not really, Lou. This guy really knows how to shop. It only cost him three dollars."

"Get the hell out of here, John. He only paid three dollars, for a combination washer-dryer?"

"That's right. He got her a douche' bag, and a towel."

"Now she can handle two loads a day. That's pretty good, for a retired lady."

"Did you know that Mary was once a school teacher? She told me a story about volunteering her service's on an Indian reservation. The tribe had a one room school house which could seat about twenty kids. The first day of school, Mary had the kids stand up and say their names. The first one up, said, Wagon-wheels. When Mary protested about him fooling around, the boy then explained that when Indian women gave birth, they named the baby after the first thing that they saw. The first thing that his mother saw was wagon wheels. Mary didn't believe him, but he insisted. She told him if he didn't tell the truth, she'd throw him out of the class. Looking frustrated, the Indian boy turned to his brother and said, 'Come on, two deer fucking. She won't believe you either."

"Some stories are hard to believe. I wonder, what's the name of that tribe?"

"Well, she said the tribe was from the tip of Long Island, somewhere near Montauk Point. She said that all the men had a peculiar abnormality, pertaining to their sexual prowess. It seems that they all had dongs that reached halfway down their legs."

"You're Kidding. What were they called?"

"They were called the Shin-a-cocks."

"I'd never make it in that tribe. You know, we should have gotten Mary a nice birthday gift, instead of just singing to her. What do you think?"

"I think its harder then it sounds. Birthday gifts never seem to work out. I remember last year, for my birthday, my wife gave me, a shirt, a new belt, and a piece of ass. And let me tell ya something, Mary, all of them were three sizes too big."

"One day," I tell the crowd, "When Gus was a little boy, he saw two dogs just like the Indian's deer, screwing in the street, and he asked his father about it. His father explained that they were making a puppy. About two weeks later, Gus walked in on Mary and her husband making love. Gus asked what they were doing, and his father yelled out, 'We're making a baby.' Gus thought it over, and then screamed, 'Turn her over, Pop...I'd rather have a puppy."

"I was told by Gus that his mother only had one student who wasn't an Indian, and that was a little Italian kid named Gino. He wanted to make a good impression so when Mary asked the class who could spell Mississippi, Gino bravely held up his hand. He took a deep breath and said, 'I'm a gonna try. Okay, M comma first, and then I come...and then two asses come a together...and then I come again... and then two asses come together again...Then I come, pee pee twice, come again...that's it, Mississippi."

"He must have been a Wop-a-ho."

"Well, whatever he was, it's still happy birthday to Mary, and I think we should at least sing her a song."

"Wait a minute, Lou. What about Suzie. She's just turned twenty-one today. We almost forgot about her."

"You're right. How could anyone forget Suzie.

155

"Maybe you guys didn't recognize her, but this young woman is a fabulous inventor."

"Oh! I remember now," I say. "Didn't she invent the wearable hair dryer that you can wear around your house as you do your cooking?"

"No, John. That's called a towel."

"Did she invent the mini-toaster that not only toasts your bread but also vacuums up the crumbs and makes an extra slice of toast out of it?"

"No Larry. That's called a wet finger. Let me ask you this, did you guys ever hear of Gonorrhea?"

"Well sure we did," we both say.

Larry, steps up to micro-phone, and says, "Are you trying to tell us that Suzie Moore, sitting right in this room, actually invented Gonorrhea?"

Lou adjusts his guitar and says, "Well, I wouldn't say that she actually invented Gonorhea, but I'll tell you this. She happens to be the sole distributor for the entire eastern seaboard."

"She's sharing with others," I announce. "It's like being married... for better or for worse."

Louie says, "You're right. Ladies and Gents, this is a special birthday song for Suzie Moore that we'd like to share with you."

"I can only guess how she got that name." All three of us chant, "More Suzie, More."

I begin a quick rhythm with the brushes, and sing,
Mary had a chicken, Suzie had a duck,
They put them on the table, to see if they would F...

"Hey," Louie interrupts, what's wrong with you. You gotta watch what you say, jeez, Mary had a chicken, Suzie had a duck..."

"Wait a minute, Lou, I was only gonna say, that they wanted to see if they would fall off."

"Oh... fall off. Now I see what you were doing. I jumped the gun. Sorry. And of course, now that I think about it, they wouldn't fall off, right?"

"Of, course not. You'd have to jerk them off."

"All right, stop it now. We're supposed to sing a nice song to Suzie. Let's get everyone to sing."

We begin an intro to the tune, *"Nothing would be finer, then to be in Carolina, in the morning.*

We make a driving rhythm for the intro, and sing.
OH! Nothing would be finer
Then to be in her vagina, in the morning,
It is like a diamond,
In the middle of her hymen, in the morning,
If your name was Cynthia,
I would crawl right into ya,
If your name was Dolores,
I would eat, your clitor....

"Hey, what's wrong with you? You can't say things like that about such a beautiful girl. Watch what you say."

"I couldn't help it Lou. It was on the tip of my tongue all night."

"I think we've been up here long enough. Mary Lombardo, we want to dedicate this last song to you. Every man should be so lucky, as to have a girl like you, at least once in their life. Of course, not every man wants a girl like you, and that's what this song is all about." The group begins softly playing the intro to *My Way*, and as Louie starts, you can hear he has a pronounced lisp.

And now, your end is near,
So I'll pull down the curtain,
My friend, I'll say it clear,
I'd like to make it with Richard Burton,
I've had my share of girls,
I've traveled each and every thigh say,
But then again, I'd rather have men,
Who'll do it my way,

Brunette's, I've had a few,
But then again, too few to matter,
I did what I had to do,
As though they were served on a platter,
I've planned each intercourse,
And then one day, I tried a guy lay,
Now I want more,
I'll take the Marine Corps,

If they'll do it my way,

For there were times, I'm sure you knew
When I bit off more then I could chew,
And through it all, when there was doubt,
I ate it up, and spit it out,
I'll take one and all, if they'll stand tall,
And, do it my way,

For what is a man, what has he got,
If he's got two inches, he's got a lot,
To feel the things he really sees,
Especially when he's on his knees,
The record shows, I took the blows,
And did it my way.

Louie announces "Happy birthday, Mary, and we hope to see you every year until we get shut down by the cops. Maybe everybody should sing happy birthday to Mary. C'mon folks, everybody sing.
Happy birthday to you,(show me your tits)
Happy birthday to you,(show me your tits)
You look just like my mudder, soooo,
Show us your tits.
"Congratulations sweetheart, and stick around. The guys are whipping something up for you in the kitchen as we speak.

Anybody who wants to get a piece of Mary's, uh, cake, please hang around. For those of you who don't give a shit about an eighty year old lady who's all alone except for her gangster son Gus, we hope to see you again, and have a great night. For those we haven't scared out of here yet, we'll see you in a while."

Lou plays the last line of '*My Way*', and the group joins in and finishes the set. The lights on the stage are switched off. The waiters scramble to get me and Larry our bar tabs. Much of the crowd stands indicating that they're going to leave. Sal blocks the door to assure that no one leaves without producing a stub showing that they've paid. The bar tenders are busy ringing up tabs and giving change. The waiters are sweeping debris from the table tops to the floor and wiping down the tables. New 'Minimum' cards are placed next to the dumped tuna cans, and as Louie exchanges words with the customer's, we get ready for another crowd. Everything happens like clock work. Not a moment is wasted. As the Juke Box goes on, someone yells out, "When's the next show gonna start?"

A waiter answers, "Take a break, big ass. Grab your girl, tell her nice things, have a drink, spend some money. Give us an hour and we'll start all over again. We're just warming up."

Chapter 24

The Cream of the Crap

That was an example of what a show was like. I can only hope that I've conveyed a real sense of the songs and the pace of the show. I realize that you couldn't smell the meatball sandwiches and the burgers and fry's, but I want you to know that the delivery of food and drinks were a good part of the nights craziness. The quality of the voices and the comedic timing is left to your imagination, but any Club that can do well for almost half a century has got to be doing something right.

The Crazy Country Club closed its doors in 1992. The reasons are varied as to its demise. Perhaps the neighborhoods changed and now the droves of Italians, Irish, and Jews have been replaced by the Russians, Mexicans and Orientals. The funny thing about this is that we've always picked on all ethnic groups to some degree. Maybe the reason we didn't focus on them as much, was because they weren't in the majority. For some reason, we always attacked our own the most. This way, no one had anything to bitch about. It wasn't a requirement that you be of Italian, Jewish, or German heritage to work at the club, it just turned out that way. Most of us were of Italian heritage and so we did more to the Italians then anyone else. It seems difficult for me to imagine a Korean doing some of the parodies that we did, although I think that could be funny as hell. I don't believe you'd find a Club filled with three hundred Asians of different ages, looking to be roasted. There's something very European about what took place because we related to our grand parents and their *accents and traditions. We knew* we could play off of that. I mean, a Jew could tell you where to get the best pizza and an Irishman would know where the tastiest Knish was made. Italians loved Polish sausage, and on and on it went. We had something to share and we did it through humor. The Puerto Ricans that frequented the Club were great sports and took it on the chin with the best of us. Again, it was their food, their dancing and accents that were so familiar to everyone. We were connected. We laughed at each other. On occasion we'd get groups of Black Americans to visit and again they were fine with the Club. I think most of our customer base was built on the logistics of the neighborhoods. Everybody was welcome at the club. We didn't care what you were. You could be a convict, a college kid, or a prostitute. Everybody created the opportunity for more humor. We loved the differences. It's funny to me that you could have a wise guy sitting next to a cop and they'd meld like a common glue had affected them. That glue was humor. I recall on two occasions, a Catholic Priests in street cloths sitting at the bar, laughing along with everyone. It was the same thing with some Rabbi. In a way it was like watching a cartoon. You see the Roadrunner trick the Coyote and you watch him fall a thousand feet to the ground. You hear the thud and see the cloud of dust, and yet you know that he really isn't hurt. The next minute, he's up and running again. That was the Club. It was never taken seriously. We weren't political and we really never hurt anyone.

I've had the opportunity to visit some comedy clubs and it seems to me the diversity that I enjoyed is gone. We had Italian, Spanish, Irish, Swedish, and you name it to work with, whereas today, you're a Black, a White or a Hispanic. The Whites are only portrayed as nerds, devoid of all the differences that made them funny. Years ago, great comics like Sid Ceasar, made a career by doing accents and highlighting everyone's quirks. It was the way America grew and accepted every new group of immigrants. I think it eased the road to acceptance, because it was built on humor. When something's funny, it doesn't hurt as much.

Today, the whites are nerds, the Spanish are either gang members or migrant workers, and the Blacks are humping instructors. If I see another black comic with bad material, humping the air I'm going to throw up. Doctor Bill Cosby must really get upset when he sees what's happening. I liked it a lot better when we were kidding each other and laughing about it. I think the idea of law suits and making an example of someone because different races are involved only makes things worse. Things are tough enough out there in the real world, so lighten up. Relax, have a drink and laugh a little. No body's forcing you to do anything.

The Club certainly left its mark. There were many that worked there that I didn't mention. I concentrated on the guys I worked with, in order to keep it short and to the point. Some of them I've lost track of and try as I may I couldn't locate them.

My brothers Carl and Andy are both retired New York City Policemen, with Andy living in New York and Carl in Florida. Little Tony, Big Dick and Stevie Shades were among those I couldn't find. Maybe if they'll read this, they'll surface again.

Johnny Nibs still lives in Brooklyn where he enjoys being a grandfather. Stewie now resides in New Jersey and is doing well. They say he hasn't changed.

My best friend Larry resides in upstate New York, in a rural area. Years ago he told me a story of what his rather quiet life was like in the boon docks.

In retirement he had put on quite a bit of weight, and he decided to get some exercise by putting in a swimming pool. The back of his house had a flat surface for about fifty feet and then turned steeply into a mountain. The driveway off of the dirt road to his house was long and deserted, providing plenty of privacy. Larry lived alone.

He erected an above ground twenty by forty foot swimming pool in his yard, with a single ladder to serve him. Once everything was in place, the pool filled and cleaned, he decided to take a swim. Being alone and in complete privacy, he decided to go skinny dipping.

He shed his cloths down to his birthday suit, and climbed the rickety ladder. Lowering himself into the water, he pushed off the side. Being a good swimmer he took a few laps and then settled onto a floating mat that he'd inflated. The water was cool and invigorating, and settling in he decided to take a snooze. He closed his eyes and relaxed. All was perfect with the world.

He's not sure if he had actually fallen asleep, or just had his eyes closed, but he suddenly felt that he wasn't alone. Opening his eyes, he scanned the pools water and seeing nothing he used his hands as a paddle and turned towards the mountain. Then he saw it. Sitting on his ass only twenty feet from the pools edge was a large black bear. He sat quietly on the steep mountain side observing Larry. Neither one of them moved. Larry, knowing that he was in a bad spot, with no weapon to protect him, went into survival mode. His mind raced.

Again he quietly and slowly paddled his way to the ladder. Knowing he had to make a move to get to his house, he climbed the rickety stairs. Turning to face the bear in order to go down the stairs safely, he stood on the top step as naked as the day he was born. He said the look on the bears face was one of bewilderment as if he'd just seen a hairless bear that was bigger then he was. Larry read the bears look as a look of freight, and roared.

Picture this scene. There's a man standing on the top rung of a pool ladder, six feet tall and well over three hundred pounds, with arms outstretched, showing his bird to a wild black bear. The bear turned and rapidly ran up the hill, as Larry high tailed his ass to the safety of his house. He didn't even have time to pick up his cloths. However, he had won again by being a quick thinker. What a story he had to tell, not to mention the bragging rights that went with his bird scaring a black bear away. He's one funny bastard.

There are others to mention. No longer with us are Cappy, Jimmy Moose, Otto, Sal Da Doorman, Crazy Tony, Pete the Bartender, and Tommy a/k/a Uncle Festus, Mister Clean. All of these guys were terrific people who really had a good time working hard for a few bucks and a lot of fun. Every one was unique. Everybody brought their own bag of tricks to the party.

Tony Burdo lives in Staten Island with his son, AJ. He still plays gigs and of course visits his father often. There was a time that Tony and his younger and crazier brother Scott, opened up a Club in Staten Island. It was based on the Country Clubs idea, with more emphasis on selling Italian style dinners. It was called *The Spaghetti Bender Café*. They erected a large sign on the awning that read, *"Eat here or we both starve."* All the cutlery was bent, nothing matched, and the place resembled the old club. The bar area was called *"Hot Nuts," and the sign* read *"You bring 'em, we break um." The menu had interesting choices as any fine restaurant would have. It read like this.*

Apperteases… Mozzarella stix-triangular shaped. (Easy to pick up, and throw.)

Fried Calamari…(to be eaten with eyes closed.)

Tender Tips (tips of what?) And on and on it went. The entire menu read like that.

The main difference to me was the help. I think I really missed seeing the Cream of the Crap serving drinks. I hungered for those one-liners that just came out of thin air. I missed the guys.

Lou Burdo has just turned 88 years old and also lives in Staten Island with his wife Pearl. His wife is a pretty petite Jewish princess with red hair and a great sense of humor. In talking on the phone with Lou recently, he related how Pearl would sometimes dance slowly with Armando, The Midget. Armando would visit the club accompanied by a few wise guys who enjoyed and protected him. He was always a great sport who found humor in his unfortunate situation. As Lou would sing a love song, they would dance slowly, nose to crotch. The place would go wild. I miss that too.

Although Louie's had his share of medical problems over the last ten years, he has still on occasion gone out with Tony and Stewie and done some shows. He's as funny as ever and you only have to talk to him to sense the comedic genius lurking there.

For many years I dreamt about writing a book about the club. I believed it forty years ago, and I still believe it today, that there should be a movie about what went on in Brooklyn. It's too rich a past with too many characters to just let it slip by. I could see Joe Pesci playing the part of Louie or maybe Paul Giamatti. They both sing and can tell a joke. I laugh when I picture Jim Carrey as Stewie, making faces and contorting his body. I see Danny Aiello as Sal Da Doorman and Chaz Palminteri as Pete the bartender. You'd have to do some searching to get someone to play Tommy, because Otto Preminger is not around anymore. *Morte'.* Brad Garrett or Steve Schirippa could be Larry and I'm sure they could find some schmuck to play me. All you need is a good casting director and you could fill all the shoes that walked the clubs floor. Oh, how I love to dream.

I guess that the long and short of this story is this. This club didn't materialize on someone's drawing board. No one sat down and designed this place with a goal to create a comedy club. There was no grand scheme in mind. This club emerged. Keep in mind that unlike comedy clubs across the country that rely solely on stand-ups to come and ply their trade, Louie relied solely on his own wits, and those that worked for him. Warm Beer and Lousy Food happened because a man was simply trying to make a living, and his personality got in the way.

The End

About the author

John Columbia was born and raised in Brooklyn New York, the eldest of seven children. He attended both Parochial and Public schools which ended for him at the age of sixteen. He served four years in The Air Force where he was actively involved in doing shows, as both a singer and a comic. Upon discharge, he worked many jobs; hairdressing, construction, Wall Street to name a few. He joined the Crazy Country Club in 1965. Frequently bitten by the entrepreneurial spirit, he and his wife Kathy have owned two beauty Parlors, and a clothing store. In 1977 he left The Crazy Country Club and joined The New York City Fire Department. He has four brothers who are retired New York City Policemen. His rich past is a source of inspiration and gives energy to his writing, his life experience running the gamut of emotions, tinged with a survivor's sense of humor. In addition to writing, he loves singing and oil painting. He has one son John, his wife Val, and two grandchildren, John and Gianna.